MW00354700

# WURLITZER ∮ CINCINNATI

## *The Name That Means Music to Millions*

**MARK PALKOVIC**

THE
History
PRESS

LIBRARY OF
CONGRESS
SURPLUS
DUPLICATE

Published by The History Press
Charleston, SC 29403
www.historypress.net

Copyright © 2015 by Mark Palkovic
All rights reserved

*Front cover*: Wurlitzer's iconic Model 1015 jukebox of 1946. *Courtesy of Gert Almind.*
*Back cover, left top*: The console of the Wurlitzer theater organ in the Riviera Theatre, North Tonawanda, New York. *Courtesy of North Tonawanda History Museum*; *right top*: Wurlitzer Style 125 military band organ of 1915. *From* The Golden Age of Automatic Musical Instruments, *copyright 2001, Arthur A. Reblitz, Mechanical Music Press. Used with permission*; *bottom*: First day cover of a first-class stamp issued by the U.S. Postal Service in 1995 to commemorate the fiftieth anniversary of the most popular jukebox in history, the Wurlitzer Model 1015. *Courtesy of Greg Dumais.*

First published 2015

Manufactured in the United States

ISBN 978.1.62619.446.5

Library of Congress Control Number: 2015932377

*Notice*: The information in this book is true and complete to the best of our knowledge. It is offered without guarantee on the part of the author or The History Press. The author and The History Press disclaim all liability in connection with the use of this book.

All rights reserved. No part of this book may be reproduced or transmitted in any form whatsoever without prior written permission from the publisher except in the case of brief quotations embodied in critical articles and reviews.

*For Tom*

# CONTENTS

# ACKNOWLEDGEMENTS

I am indebted to many people who provided information and support in the preparation of this book. Cincinnati-area organ technician and Wurlitzer aficionado Ron Wehmeier provided me with valuable leads and other information about the Wurlitzer Company and its theater organs in particular; Philip Groshong provided photographs of Wehmeier and his Wurlitzer instruments. William E. Greiss Jr., a great-grandson of Rudolph Wurlitzer, proved invaluable in verifying and providing information and photos of the Wurlitzer family. Gert J. Almind, editor of the Danish Jukebox Archives, provided me with much information about Wurlitzer's jukebox production and models, along with images. Donna Zellner Neal, executive director of the North Tonawanda History Museum provided valuable information and graciously allowed me unfettered access to the museum's holdings, including images from the collection. Tom Austen, current owner of the main portion of the former Wurlitzer North Tonawanda factory, provided information about the building and conducted a tour of the facility. Louis Rosa, former employee at the North Tonawanda factory, provided photos of harp manufacturing. I am also indebted to Margret Abbott, assistant university archivist at the Regional History Center of Northern Illinois University; Kay Peterson, customer service representative of the Archives Center, National Museum of American History, Smithsonian Institution; and Diane Mallstrom, reference librarian at the Public Library of Cincinnati and Hamilton County. Bernadette Rubbo and Vonda K. Givens of the Stickley Museum at Craftsman Farms provided images of the Stickley/Farny house there. Jeff Weiler, Art Reblitz and Ron Bopp gave permission to use images from their collections. Heather Moore, photo historian at the U.S. Senate Historical Office provided an image of Senator Homer Capehart. I am greatly indebted to Elizabeth Caminiti of the Gibson Guitar Corporation, current owner of the Wurlitzer brand, for granting me permission to reproduce Wurlitzer advertising and logos. Unless otherwise noted, images are from the author's collection or Wurlitzer. Finally, I thank Greg Dumais, commissioning editor at The History Press, for his invaluable help in seeing this book through to completion.

# INTRODUCTION

A significant historical source used here to recount the history of the Wurlitzer and Farny families and the first one hundred years of the Rudolph Wurlitzer Company is a typewritten manuscript completed in 1955 by Lloyd Graham (1893–1991). Graham was a professional writer active in the Niagara Falls and Buffalo, New York area and was apparently hired by Wurlitzer at the time of the company's centennial to record this information in narrative form. Other writers and family members agree that Graham extensively interviewed Farny Wurlitzer, the only child of Rudolph Wurlitzer alive at the time, who would have known the specific facts and could provide the physical records to allow Graham to compile his text.

Farny and Grace Wurlitzer had no children, but Farny had his secretary update a roster whenever a new grandniece or grandnephew was born, when marriages took place and at the deaths of nephews and nieces. Every year for Christmas, Uncle Farny sent each of the thirty-eight grandnieces and grandnephews a greeting in an envelope with a fancy seal containing a five-dollar bill. When they were old enough to have children of their own, Uncle Farny continued the tradition with his great-grandnieces and nephews.

It is obvious that Farny had a family spirit. One such letter from him dated December 11, 1951, states

> *For a long time I have been thinking of bringing the memory of great-grandfather and great-grandmother Wurlitzer a little closer to each of their thirty-eight great-grandchildren, as none of the thirty-eight knew*

*their great-grandfather and only a few have recollections of their great-grandmother. Your great-grandparents had most unusual and interesting lives and made such sacrifices that we all can be grateful and proud of their strong and upright characters which brought success to them and greater opportunities to us than we would otherwise have enjoyed. Some time in the future I intend to write, with the help of your Aunt Sylvia and others in the family, the story of their lives, and will send it to you when completed.*

Graham's writing is apparently the fulfillment of Farny's plan. Although various research resources verified most facts as set forth by Graham, some of his narrative contains facts or situations that were impossible to verify elsewhere. Since Graham worked directly with Farny, we can assume that his writing is accurate. However, there are discrepancies in a number of statements, dates, dollar amounts and so forth regarding the early history of the family and the company. In these instances, I compared Graham's writing to other resources (see Bibliography) to determine the most likely reality; however, much of the section of the present book regarding the family and the early years of the company is presented here with little or no change from Graham's work. Likewise, for the section on Wurlitzer organs, I relied heavily on Jeff Weiler's excellent research in his book *The Wurlitzer Pipe Organ* edited by David L. Junchen, presented here with only minor editorial changes.

Although for much of its existence the Wurlitzer Company was headquartered in Cincinnati, there is little source material available in libraries and archives there. In 1941, the company headquarters were moved to Chicago; in 1976, Wurlitzer again relocated its main office, this time to DeKalb, Illinois, the site of its piano factory from 1919 to 1973. Anticipating its sale, in 1984, Wurlitzer donated its records and other archival material to the Regional History Center and University Archives at Northern Illinois University in DeKalb. Eight years later, the majority of this material was transferred to the Smithsonian Institution's National Museum of American History in Washington, D.C. The North Tonawanda History Museum in North Tonawanda, New York, also contains a wealth of information and source material, including specimens of many of the products manufactured by Wurlitzer at its North Tonawanda factory. Across Webster Street from the museum is the Riviera Theatre, which contains a Wurlitzer theater organ originally installed there in 1927. This instrument was often played by or for

Wurlitzer customers when visiting the factory to arrange for the design, construction and purchase of a theater organ for another venue. The Riviera's organ has been restored in recent years, but it has almost continuously provided entertainment to audiences and continues to do so today.

The sheer variety and quantity of items sold or manufactured by Wurlitzer during its 150-year existence reveal it to be an American success story. I hope that within these pages you will discover why Wurlitzer was "the name that means music to millions."

# 1
# RUDOLPH WURLITZER

Cincinnati was taking its place on the national stage in the mid-1800s. The Democratic National Convention took place here in June 1856, nominating James Buchanan for president instead of the incumbent president, Franklin Pierce. Buchanan's election to the office of president later that year helped set in motion events leading up to the Civil War. The winter of 1856–57 was so cold that the Ohio River froze solid from the Kentucky shore to Ohio, enabling an additional entry point to the North for escaping slaves on the Underground Railroad. Harriet Beecher Stowe's influential novel *Uncle Tom's Cabin* was inspired by that and similar events she saw or heard about while living here.

During times of such political and social turmoil, people often turn to artistic diversions such as music to take their minds off their troubles; thus, music played a significant role in the life of Cincinnati. In the early 1800s, Cincinnati was a destination for German immigration, and among the many customs and sensibilities the Germans brought to the city was a love of music. In his 1864 book, Emil Klauprecht said, "To the Americans belongs the credit of being the first pioneers of music in Cincinnati; but the Germans may boast of having brought about its higher development."

In 1849, a number of small German singing societies met together to establish a larger organization similar to those already in place in Bavaria and other parts of Germany in order to foster good fellowship through singing. This led to the formation of the German Saengerbund of North America and the establishment of periodic singing festivals. The May

On September 24, 1848, Charles Fontayne and William S. Porter took a series of panoramic photographs of Cincinnati from a rooftop across the Ohio River in Newport, Kentucky. It is one of the oldest photographs of an urban area in existence. Shown here is Plate Four, looking up Lawrence Street; at the end of the street is the Jacob Strader House on Fourth Street. Cincinnati appeared much this way when Rudolph Wurlitzer arrived here five years later. *From the collection of the Public Library of Cincinnati and Hamilton County.*

Festival of choral music was first held in Cincinnati in 1873 and continues to be held annually today.

One of the many men who rode the wave of German immigration to the city was Franz Rudolph Wurlitzer. He embraced the American dream and created a successful musical instrument business with a worldwide reputation. He was born January 30, 1831, in the Saxony village of Schöneck in an area of rolling hills and well-kept farms with thrifty, hardworking citizens.

Rudolph's father, Christian, had an older half-brother, Karl, who had inherited the family estate and occupied a property of two thousand acres in farms and woodland about a mile and a half from Schöneck. Rudolph's uncle Karl lived a full century, passing on in 1900. He had no children, and surprisingly, he left all of his property to a farmhand who had worked for him the last seven years of his life. For years, there had been bad feelings between Christian and Karl, a bitterness that had roots in the traditions of German family life and property ownership. In the German tradition of the day, the rule of primogeniture was unquestioned. The estate, the prized family possessions and the honors and the titles thus descended from the father to the eldest son. Christian Wurlitzer resented that his half-brother had inherited the family estate.

Nevertheless, Christian established himself as a successful businessman in his own right. By 1853, he had built up a prosperous business and become a man of property, operating a large general store. Christian Wurlitzer obtained musical instruments and lace from the skilled craftsmen in the area and in turn sold these people groceries, clothing and other necessities.

Rudolph became uncomfortably aware of the depth of the difficult relationship between his father, Christian, and his uncle Karl after completing his education. As a young boy, he had attended the village school in Schöneck. He then went to school in Plauen, Saxony, and followed this with study at the Commercial Institution in Schweinfurt, Bavaria. There is evidence that Rudolph also attended the Händelschule in Leipzig.

As the eldest son, Rudolph returned to Schöneck after graduation with the hope of inheriting his father's prosperous business, but in the early summer of 1853, matters reached a crisis. Rudolph's father was now forty-six years old, having been born on February 19, 1807, in Schöneck. On August 19, 1830, Christian had married a village girl, Christiane Fredericka Hochmuth almost exactly three years younger. With Rudolph as the eldest child, Christian and Christiane Fredericka had a large family that included their other children: Henriette Adelheid, Auguste Amalie, Fredericka Marie, Franz Anton, Wilhelm Constantin, Agnes Marthe, Agnes Bertha, Constantin and Paul Albert, the last. Four of the children—Paul Albert, Wilhelm Constantin, Agnes Marthe and Agnes Bertha—failed to survive infancy.

However, Rudolph's hopes of joining his father in business were dashed when he learned that, although Christian would like to have him in the business, he wanted Rudolph only as a paid employee. Even though Rudolph was the eldest son, he could expect no advantages or favors and would never be an owner. Because of his experience with his half-brother Karl, Christian was determined to handle the question of inheritance quite differently in his family, planning to reverse the order of inheritance and ensuring that his youngest son, not the eldest, would inherit his estate.

Rudolph was shocked. Constantin, the youngest surviving son, was then only six years old, and Franz Anton was only fourteen. Christian's radical ideas of inheritance meant that Rudolph could go to work in the business, spend his life there, and Constantin, who could not possibly take his part in the business for another fifteen or sixteen years, would reap the fruits of his eldest brother's labor. Eventually, the business would belong to Constantin.

Rudolph refused to accept his father's decision of inheritance, which surprised Christian. When asked by his father what he would do instead of working in the family business, Rudolph stated his decision to go to America.

After all, stories were filtering back to Saxony about Germans who had emigrated and established a good life there.

Christian knew that Rudolph had no money of his own. He expected the matter to drop when Rudolph realized this, but Christian soon found that he was dealing with a son who was as determined and as assertive as he was. And Rudolph had the support of his mother's side of the family.

Christiane, Rudolph's mother, had died five years earlier, on July 17, 1848. Little is known of her, but on February 29, 1848, she wrote a letter to her son who was away at school.

> *I now will explain my hopes for you, that I shall have good news from you and that you will have fine, good, and thrifty friends that will influence you, so that you will know how to handle a grosch* [money]. *You know how much faith I have in you and how I have to act towards the children for your sake. Please try hard to find a place to stay and good work, then I'll be able to live happily and die in peace. Love, your Mother.*

Rudolph talked with his mother's brother, Uncle Wilhelm Hochmuth, about his determination to cut loose from his father and see how he could do in America. Uncle Wilhelm was touched. After all, this was his dead sister's child, her favorite and the one for whom she had had such high hopes. Uncle Wilhelm consequently loaned his nephew the relatively large sum of 350 marks (about 80 dollars), and the decision was made. This was a big step for Rudolph, just twenty-one years old and small for his age, only five feet, four inches tall.

So, with 350 marks in his pocket, young Rudolph Wurlitzer bought passage for America and set out in 1853 with the few belongings he could carry. He was determined to repay Uncle Wilhelm Hochmuth's loan as soon as he could. He was also determined to succeed in America. His bridges were burned, and he could not face his father in defeat. He made the decision that he would save the first one-quarter of anything he earned.

Shortly after his arrival in America, young Rudolph Wurlitzer found his first job, working for a Hoboken grocer in New Jersey for long hours and very little pay. His first experiences in America must have been very disillusioning. The crowded, cobbled streets of Hoboken were a long, long way from the green hills and familiar slow pace of life in Schöneck. His command of the English language was rudimentary, and he was often the butt of jokes and laughter from the women who shopped in the grocery. Soon after, he moved on to Philadelphia.

But the City of Brotherly Love did not live up to its name for Rudolph. As just one of many young immigrant men seeking a job, he stopped a well-dressed Philadelphian on the street, intending to ask him if he knew where he could find work. But before he could ask his question, the man cut him off and chastised him for being a beggar and a contemptible foreign beggar at that.

Humiliated by this treatment, Rudolph decided to leave Philadelphia. A friend told him of greater opportunities in Cincinnati, and he decided to make his way there. Cincinnati at this time and for many years to come was a destination for German immigrants.

From the start, Cincinnati was hospitable to him, and at first, he earned a living by peddling articles door to door. But he was much more ambitious than that. He quickly found a job as porter in a dry goods establishment at a wage of four dollars per week. In order to be able to save the quarter of his earnings that he had promised himself, he reduced his living expenses by receiving permission from his employer to sleep in a packing case on the property.

He soon found better a better job with the Cincinnati dry goods merchant and banking house of Heidelbach and Seasongood, earning eight dollars per week plus the privilege, at first, of sleeping in a loft over the banking offices.

Heidelbach and Seasongood found the young man honest and industrious. He learned American ways and the English language faster than most boys from the old country, and his employer promoted him steadily. There is no doubt that this position with the banking house offered opportunities that he otherwise would not have been exposed to. And he did have an eye for opportunity.

It is impossible to determine now exactly what Rudolph did in those early Cincinnati days, but there is reason to believe that at the end of the first three years in America, young Rudolph Wurlitzer had repaid his passage expenses to Uncle Wilhelm Hochmuth and had accumulated a modest amount of money. However, there is no proof as to the exact figure, and it is obvious that he could not have saved much money from his job at Heidelbach and Seasongood.

Family lore has it that he was briefly involved in the purchase and export of native products such as ginseng root dug in the Kentucky mountains and exported to China; the purchase of mink, raccoon and opossum furs in the Ohio Valley and sold at a profit in Antwerp and Amsterdam; and the acquisition of semiprecious stones brought in from the mountains of North Carolina and Tennessee and shipped by young Rudolph Wurlitzer to the gem markets of Amsterdam. It is likely that at least some of these ventures were made in association with others. Although these ventures brought in much-needed funds, their speculative nature was likely too risky to appeal to him in the long term since his personality was essentially canny, hardworking and thrifty. He needed a more stable way of making money, so he decided to focus on the musical instruments manufactured back in his homeland.

Young Rudolph Wurlitzer did not play any musical instrument himself, but he loved music and found great enjoyment in listening to it. His hometown of Schöneck was in the center of a considerable musical instrument business. Essentially an agrarian society, these were people who lived off the land but kept profitably busy during the winter months by making violins and woodwind instruments. Their crops kept them occupied during the summers. The cottage industry of making musical instruments was quite specialized and well organized. The men of several families sometimes worked together to make musical instruments, each specializing in certain parts. The Wurlitzer family has been identified with making or dealing in musical instruments in one way or another for 350 years.

From his boyhood, Rudolph was familiar with musical instruments, having grown up in the musical instrument business. Nearly every family in Schöneck had one or more men who knew how to make violins or other instruments. His father had built up a good business dealing in musical instruments made in the homes of his Schöneck neighbors, and Rudolph himself had worked in this business.

The region is sometimes referred to today as "Musicon Valley," and its central town is Markneukirchen, where violin maker Ludwig Gläsel Jr. (1842–1931) plied his trade and famously labeled his violins as being made in the town sometimes called the "German Cremona." This reveals the high regard in which the instruments were held. Today, there are still 113 businesses in the area that are involved in the manufacture of musical instruments.

The Musikinstrumenten Museum Markneukirchen was founded in 1883 by Paul Otto Apian-Bennewitz, a teacher and organist. The collection, designed to be a teaching collection of European and ethnic instruments, now includes more than 3,100 items from Europe, Asia, Africa, America and Australia. However, the core collection consists of instruments from the immediate area and documents their development from the seventeenth century to the present. The museum has a violin that is a fine example of the work of Hanuss Adam Wurlitzer, a member of the Violin Makers Guild.

Rudolph's ancestors Johannes Wurlitzer, born 1628, and his son, Michael, were lute makers. Michael's son, Hanuss Andreas, born in 1701, and his nephew, Hanuss Adam Wurlitzer, were the first violin makers in the family.

Johan Andreas, born August 8, 1771, the father of Christian Gottfried Wurlitzer, Rudolph's father, was a son of Hanuss Andreas, the younger, born 1732. The church registry of Markneukirchen refers to Johann Adam Wurlitzer, who is described as a bass-violin maker. All of them were involved in the production or sale of musical instruments.

The economic progress of these early musical instrument craftsmen was slow but steady. Tax records of the seventeenth century show that all of them owned the houses they lived in. They displayed and sold their instruments at fairs, markets and cultural centers. They used the pine and maple from the local forests of upper Vogtland; later, they also used choice woods that grew in the Alps, Bavaria and the Carpathians.

Beginning about 1700, these musical instrument makers prospered. The Markneukirchen craftsmen branched out into the production of percussion instruments and woodwinds as well as stringed instruments in addition to violins, producing practically everything that an orchestra might need. By 1820, more than three hundred persons, not including wives and children, were occupied making all kinds of musical instruments in this area, and the instruments were finding owners all over the world.

Down through the years, the craftsmen and dealers in Markneukirchen were leaders in musical innovations. They organized a "Sunday School" for theoretical and practical instruction in music in 1834. The trade union was organized in 1872, the instrument-building school in 1878 and the Exhibition of Trade and Industry in 1897.

Thus, young Rudolph Wurlitzer came from a long tradition of musical instrument manufacturing and selling. It would have been surprising if he had *not* become engaged in the musical instrument business in America. It was fortunate that conditions were ideal in Cincinnati for him to enter the field.

# 2
# How the Business Began

Cist's *Sketches and Statistics of Cincinnati in 1851* lists eighty-two musicians, two music dealers and six musical instrument makers. Pianos were made in Cincinnati on a small scale by two makers employing a total of four persons. A factory making organs, melodeons and reed organs employed twelve persons. The firm of W.C. Peters and Sons published musical works on paper that was also made in Cincinnati.

Horace Greeley wrote in his *New York Daily Tribune* after visiting Cincinnati in 1850,

> It requires no keenness of observation to perceive that Cincinnati is destined to become the focus and mart for the grandest circle of manufacturing on this continent. Her delightful climate; her unequaled and ever-increasing facilities for cheap and rapid commercial intercourse with all parts of the country and the world; her enterprising and energetic population; her own elastic and exulting youth; are all elements which predict and insure [sic] her electric progress to giant greatness.

Cincinnati in 1856 was making its mark as a city of expanding culture and of manufacturing and trade. The 1856 Democratic National Convention, held June 2–6 at Smith and Nixon's Hall in Cincinnati, was the first national party nominating convention outside the original thirteen states. The party nominated James Buchanan of Pennsylvania for U.S. president, denying renomination for the incumbent president, Franklin Pierce. John C.

Breckinridge of Kentucky was nominated as vice president to complete the ticket.

An interesting side note is that the Smith and Nixon Piano Company, in whose facility the convention was held, was founded in 1843 and was one Cincinnati's premier piano manufacturers in the late nineteenth and early twentieth centuries. They were out of business by 1931 due to the Great Depression.

As an ambitious young man familiar with the musical instrument culture of his native Saxony, Rudolph Wurlitzer investigated the state of the musical instrument business in his adopted city of Cincinnati. Though he was not a musician himself, he could talk musical instruments with anyone.

Cincinnati businesses in 1856 included a music dealership owned by a Mr. Johnson. His store was located on the north side of Fourth Street, between Main and Walnut Streets in the same building where Smith and Nixon later operated a piano store. Wurlitzer struck up an acquaintance with a clerk in Johnson's store. Rudolph could see for himself that Johnson was short on certain types of instruments, particularly woodwinds, flutes, piccolos and clarinets.

The talkative clerk noted the fact that woodwind instruments were very difficult to obtain at the time. Wurlitzer continued to learn as much as he could about the supply and demand of musical instruments in Cincinnati. Satisfied that the clerk knew what he was talking about, young Rudolph Wurlitzer then made the decision to get into the musical instrument business.

He decided to invest $700 of his hard-earned American money to try to satisfy some of the demand in the Cincinnati market. He knew that he could quickly obtain certain musical instruments directly from the makers in Saxony. So he sent $700 to his people in Saxony,

Young Rudolph Wurlitzer. *From* Immigrant Entrepreneurship: German-American Business Biographies 1720 to the Present.

most likely to his father (with whom he was now on good terms) with instructions to ship musical instruments to him. For all practical purposes, this order was the beginning of the Rudolph Wurlitzer Company.

In a few months, this first order of instruments arrived in Cincinnati, instruments made by his friends and relatives back in the countryside around Schöneck. Wurlitzer figured his costs (including customs duty and freight), added 100 percent for profit, priced his instruments and took samples to show to Mr. Johnson.

His prospective customer examined the samples with interest. However, after being told the prices, Johnson's attitude changed. Rudolph was surprised to learn that Johnson was convinced that the instruments had been stolen; otherwise, they would not be priced so low. He informed Wurlitzer that it would be absolutely impossible for the young salesman to sell the instruments to him at the prices asked if they had been honestly acquired. Doing some quick thinking, young Rudolph confessed that since this was his first attempt at importing musical instruments, he might have made a mistake in figuring his costs.

He explained that this was a personal venture of his and that he had regular employment at Heidelbach and Seasongood's bank. He assured Johnson that the owner Philip Heidelbach knew about this venture and that he came by the instruments honestly. He promised to ask Mr. Heidelbach to speak with Johnson and vouch for him.

With that, Rudolph recalculated his costs, and with the assistance of banker Heidelbach, he succeeded in convincing Mr. Johnson that the instruments he offered had not been involved in any illicit transactions. He explained that he had not included enough to cover customs and transportation costs. He refigured his costs so well that he made $1,500 on his investment of $700. "From that time," he often said in later years, "my prices were really honest." He was on his way to success in business.

Almost immediately, Rudolph sent off $7,000 to Saxony for another shipment of musical instruments. When they were about to arrive, he rented a small room on the top floor of the Masonic Building at the northwest corner of Fourth and Sycamore Streets to warehouse them. Banker Heidelbach was supportive of Rudolph's new business plans and allowed him to continue his employment at the bank while devoting all his free time to his own musical instrument business.

It was not long before the second order was sold. Rudolph's success caused a stir back in Schöneck, contributing his share to the myth that practically everything in America glittered with gold. Rudolph Wurlitzer had become

In 1856, Rudolph Wurlitzer rented warehouse space on the fourth floor of the Masonic Building at Fourth and Sycamore Streets in Cincinnati. This was the company's birthplace and would be its home for the next three years. *Wurlitzer Company Records, Archives Center, National Museum of American History, Smithsonian Institution.*

prosperous in America in a matter of only three or four years. His father, Christian, who had been skeptical, now proudly described his son's success in America to all his friends.

Next, Rudolph bought a third and much larger supply of musical instruments from the native craftsmen. He now knew that he could easily sell at a profit all the instruments that he would care to handle, and he realized now that Mr. Johnson had had good reason to be suspicious of his first offerings. Until now, German-made musical instruments had taken a circuitous route in reaching the hands of American musicians.

In the regular channels of trade, the country craftsmen sold their instruments to local shops, such as that owned by Rudolph's father in Schöneck. The local shopkeeper sold them to a quantity dealer in one of several large German cities such as Leipzig. These dealers were the source of supply for exporters

at the German ports of Hamburg and Bremen. Exporters in turn sold their wares to American importers who sold them to wholesalers who then contacted dealers such as Johnson in Cincinnati. At each step along the line, a profit was taken.

To put it another way, Rudolph had broken the chain of trade and flew in the face of convention. Because of his knowledge of home conditions on the one hand and his understanding of the American need for musical instruments on the other, he had short-circuited the line of trade that had evolved over the past century. He had performed an economic service for the music lovers of his adopted country, and he had performed no mean service for his craftsmen friends in Saxony in broadening their market by simplifying the distribution of their fine musical instruments. He was using the best traditions of competition in a capitalistic economy.

When Rudolph returned from his first visit back to his homeland, probably in 1868, he opened a place of business upstairs at 123 Main Street, Cincinnati. This was still strictly a wholesale business, and he continued in his bank position,

The House of Wurlitzer in 1875, at 123 Main Street. *From Illustrated Cincinnati: A Pictorial Hand-book of the Queen City.*

which now was that of cashier. Cincinnati addresses were renumbered about 1895, so addresses before that time do not indicate address locations today. The first store at 123 Main Street and the next one at 115 Main Street were both located in the present-day block of Main Street between Third and Fourth Streets.

Sometime during 1859, Rudolph Wurlitzer had developed his musical instrument business to the point that it was safe for him to leave his position as cashier of the bank and devote all of his time to his own venture. By 1862, he occupied the entire building at 123 Main Street, still as a wholesaler. And his younger brother by eight years, Franz Anton Wurlitzer, had joined him in Cincinnati.

Rudolph became an American citizen on October 8, 1859. He tried to enlist in the Union army in the War Between the States, but he was rejected because of his short stature. His brother Franz Anton, however, did serve in the Union army and was wounded in action.

Rudolph began manufacturing musical instruments for the first time during the war. He saw the need for drums and trumpets in the rapidly expanding army and filled government contracts by supplying these items.

Wurlitzer manufactured drums in Cincinnati for the Spanish-American War in 1898. *Wurlitzer Company Records, Archives Center, National Museum of American History, Smithsonian Institution.*

Wurlitzer's drum logo, showing "RWB" for "Rudolph Wurlitzer and Brother." Rudolph's brother Anton was a partner in the firm from 1862 to 1890. *Courtesy of Decals Unlimited.*

At this time, he also first began to sell musical instruments at retail. When Rudolph's brother Anton got out of the army and recovered from his wound, he returned to the store as a clerk. In 1872, Rudolph took Anton in as a partner. The Cincinnati directory of that year reports the business name as "Rudolph Wurlitzer & Brother."

Although the date is unclear, it is also certain that Rudolph's youngest surviving brother, Constantin, came over to America and worked for several years as a clerk in the Wurlitzer store in Cincinnati. Unlike Anton, however, he never became a partner. Known familiarly as "Constance" in the family, Constantin never seems to have enjoyed a close relationship with Rudolph, probably because he entered into a marriage that his eldest brother heartily disapproved of.

Two logos used on Wurlitzer pianos. *Courtesy of Decals Unlimited.*

The fact that Constantin left Schöneck and came to America seems to have ruined the father's plans to hand down his business and estate in Schöneck to the youngest son, as he told Rudolph he planned to do in that fateful summer of 1853. Christian Wurlitzer was to see his own dreams dashed as all three of his sons grew up and departed to make their fortunes in America. With his plans gone awry, he must have been a lonely man when he died on June 30, 1871.

The *Cincinnati City Guide and Business Directory* of 1870 shows that the Wurlitzer business was then located at 115 Main Street, and Rudolph Wurlitzer's residence was listed as 135 Smith Street. Rudolph Wurlitzer had married Leonie Farny on September 19, 1868, and the Smith Street address was their first home. The wedding was a quiet one, held in the bride's home with only a few members of the family present. Pastor August Kroell of a German Lutheran church performed the ceremony and signed the marriage certificate. (Rudolph had been brought up in the Evangelical Lutheran faith.)

Their first child, Sylvia, was born on Smith Street on September 21, 1869. They lived briefly on Sycamore Street between Franklin and Webster, but by 1872, they had moved to a larger home at 60 Franklin Street (later renamed Woodward), where all of their other children were born.

In retrospect, Rudolph Wurlitzer's marriage to Leonie Farny was significant as the event in his life second only in importance to his decision to leave Schöneck and try to make his way in America. His young wife also came from a talented, ambitious and energetic immigrant family.

# 3
# The Farny Family

Rudolph's wife, Leonie, was the daughter of Charles and Jeannette Farny and was born on October 22, 1842, in Ribeauvillé, Alsace, France, very near the border with Germany.

Charles Farny, Leonie's father, was an idealist and a social reformer. He was born in Illhaeusern, France, on February 20, 1811, the son of François and Catherine Beschlin Farny. In 1840, he married Jeannette Weigand from a Roman Catholic family. Charles was almost thirty years old when he married Jeannette, who was a widow. He had served in the army, but after he was married, he acquired a reputation as an architect and a builder of finely made stairways and interiors, particularly for churches. At first, Charles occupied the shop space used by Ensemann, his wife's deceased first husband.

Eventually, he designed and built his own house in Ribeauvillé, with a workshop in the rear. Charles was handsome, energetic and hot-tempered. He had the foresight to build a hiding place for himself in his new home above and behind a fireplace whose entrance was covered by a painting.

Charles Farny was known in the community as a Red, a supporter of democratic government for the French people, and separation from the repressive government then in power. He made speeches in Ribeauvillé in support of the Republican ideal. (He and his followers were called Reds because, as a symbol of their political ideas, they wore bearskin caps with red linings. When attending meetings, they wore the caps inside out.) Charles viewed Catholics as his enemies because they supported Louis Phillippe, "the King of the French." And yet he married a Catholic.

Jeannette was not an active Catholic, however, and did not attend any church. She and Charles made an agreement that if their first child were a boy, all of their children would be raised in the Protestant faith; if a girl, all would be raised Catholics. Eugene was their first child, born on April 2, 1841, so all of the children were raised as Protestants.

Charles's activities in the liberal movement must have been a trial to Jeannette, but apparently, she did not complain. Charles had developed a prosperous business and a reputation for his architectural and woodcarving skills. But in his work to support the liberal cause, he essentially threw it all away.

Once, when there was a warrant out for his arrest because of his political activities, Charles found it necessary to hide in the secret compartment he had built in his house. He had to flee to Switzerland at least once until the furor over his agitation for the liberal cause had died down. Many in the community were embittered toward Charles and made his life miserable.

He was eventually told by the Catholic clergy that his persecution would stop if he and his wife would take up the church of his wife's upbringing and if they would educate their children in the Catholic schools. Charles and Jeannette both rejected this offer, even though they knew that this meant that they would have to move either to Switzerland or to America. In the end, they chose America.

The Charles Farnys sailed from Le Havre in September 1853. The family included their three sons—Eugene, twelve years old; Henri, six; and Charles, a toddling baby of a year and a half—one daughter, Leonie, eleven years old; and Jeannette's inseparable sister, Josephine. The Farny party had to carry their own supplies and food for the journey. They landed in New York on October 25, but the hardship of the voyage resulted in the death of the baby Charles two days after they arrived.

Charles's old friend Dr. Greiner urged him to settle in New York, pointing out that the city had many cultural advantages comparable to those they had known in France and warned Charles of the difficulties of everyday life beyond the East Coast. But Charles refused to listen.

Marie Farny, Charles's sister, had immigrated five years earlier with David Riddlesburgher, a stepbrother. They made it as far as western Pennsylvania, where Marie married David Bucher, also an Alsatian. Charles had heard good things about the area from his sister, so he moved his family to a settlement about ten miles from Warren. He thought this was just the place for him and his family to start life over again. He could look forward, he thought, to a simple life that would be healthy for his family as well as for himself. He had no way of knowing how wrong he could be about this.

On the way to their new home, the Farny children were fascinated by what they saw from the train windows and listened attentively to the tales of other passengers. Among those passengers were two former Alsatians returning from New York to the stores in the backwoods for which they had been buying. Henri, six, sketched scenes and characters in a little book he had kept throughout the journey. They were all shocked by the story one of the Alsatians told about an Indian who had been put off that very train by a conductor a few weeks earlier. He had paid his fare, but the conductor disliked Indians and refused to permit him to ride. In a blind fury of resentment at the injustice of the white man, the Indian had gone to a nearby farmhouse and killed the two women and six children whom he found there.

Once they arrived at their destination, Charles was eager to get established in the new life. His brother-in-law, David Bucher, proposed that they become partners in operating a sawmill on Tionesta Creek.

Living was primitive and a struggle on Tionesta Creek. The first winter in the new land was difficult enough, but their trying experience was complicated by the fact that Jeannette Farny bore a daughter, Marguerite, on December 3, 1854, a cold night with the wilderness experiencing its first large snowfall. Unable to get medical help in time, Jeannette turned to medical books that she had brought from France. The information contained in the books proved to be lifesaving for her family as well as for the neighbors and nearby Seneca Indians. Jeannette gained a reputation as a healer.

There were occasional encounters with bears and panthers, and wolves continually attacked the livestock. One autumn, their sheep got into the laurel, ate it and died. Late one winter, a hired man was driving a team of oxen home from Warren with a load of supplies. While he was crossing the Allegheny River, the ice began to break up and his sled-load of supplies began to sink. He quickly cut away one of the oxen and struggled ashore with it through the icy water, abandoning the sled, supplies, and the other ox to the river. The man was lucky to escape alive.

Schooling also proved to be difficult. Miss Kelly, a Warren schoolteacher, came out to the settlement and stayed in the Farny house during the summers after school closed. At first, the Farnys struggled with the English language, which made it difficult to buy provisions. With his characteristic energy and enthusiasm, Charles Farny set out to master the language or, at least, the dialect spoken in the backwoods of Pennsylvania. However, neither Jeannette nor her sister, Josephine, ever did succeed in speaking English well.

Frontier life brought about changes in the physical condition of the Charles Farny family. Their daughter Leonie had been ill and frail as a small child, with what was later thought to be a form of tuberculosis or scrofula affecting her eyes and spine. Her condition was serious enough that Jeannette took her little daughter to a doctor in Strassburg, who prescribed a treatment that included a dosage of cod liver oil. He said that if she were cured, she would probably be her healthiest and strongest child, and his prediction proved true. Frontier life agreed with Leonie. She became healthy and strong and very attractive as she matured.

On the other hand, her father, Charles Farny, the rugged, starry-eyed idealist who had embarked on the new and simple life with such eagerness and high spirits, found the going too difficult for him. His discouragement was mainly due to the unfortunate business partnership with his brother-in-law, David Bucher. Bucher was stingy, hard-fisted, loudmouthed and difficult. His wife, Marie, was no better. If anything, Charles found his sister, Marie, more difficult to get along with than her husband. The Buchers lived a few miles away and fed the area lumbermen at a profit. It was difficult to get domestic help, and Aunt Marie often wheedled Leonie into coming to her place to bake bread a week at a time for her huge household.

After six years of frontier hardships and difficulties with the Buchers, Charles Farny decided to give up the "simple life" and try for a better life in Cincinnati. He was familiar with the city because each spring during the years in the woods, he had been one of the party that rafted logs down the Allegheny and Ohio Rivers to Cincinnati for sale there.

The actual breaking point came when his son Eugene tried to lift a log that was too heavy for him and alarmed everyone with a hemorrhage of his lungs. Rather than go south, as advised by the doctor who treated Eugene, Charles decided to take his family to Cincinnati. In the late winter of 1859, the Farny family built rafts for the trip. The rafts were huge, with cabins for living quarters, as well as pens for chickens, horses and cows. Such rafts could be floated to Cincinnati only when the streams were swollen in springtime, a leisurely journey of six weeks. During the course of the trip, they tied up the raft at night and, from time to time, for longer periods to allow the cows and horses to go ashore and graze and the chickens to scratch.

Little is known of the Farnys' first years in Cincinnati beyond the fact that they rented rooms at Pleasant and Findlay Streets and, two years later, bought a house on McMicken Street. In September 1859, eldest son Eugene wrote a letter to a friend back in Warren saying that he was employed "in a House of Commerce" located at the steamboat landing until that day, the twenty-first, when he quit to "enter a college to learn accounting." Eugene worked at the steamboat landing from seven to ten o'clock in the morning and from four to six o'clock in the afternoon. The rest of the time, he was employed by a hops and French wine merchant, and he planned to stay in this job until he finished his studies.

Eugene promised this friend in the letter that if he visited Cincinnati, he would be able to entertain him "with some excellent juice of October for there is already quite a bit this autumn. We are already offering some of the new lot which sells for 60 cents a gallon and you can see it's too bad that I can't put a gallon in this letter which would permit you to both read and drink at the same time."

In the letter, Eugene also noted that

> *Cincinnati is quite a different place than Tionesta. One is able to amuse himself in a great variety of ways without much expense. If one likes to drink, it is possible to buy whiskey for around 23 cents a gallon, beer for about 5 cents a quart, and, at the moment, new wine costs 60 to 70 cents per gallon.*
>
> *There are a great many public libraries here in Cincinnati where one is able to read all kinds of books and papers from the entire world. Each day, it is my practice to visit one of the libraries. You can tell Mr. Remy that there are daily receipts in this library of the* Review of Two Worlds, The Courier of the United States, *etc., etc. There are also many French books of all sorts, as well as newspapers. There are [sic] the* Belgium Independence, *also many English and German newspapers. There are literally newspapers from all parts of the world as well as magazines and journals. As far as theatres, there is an English opera and two German, providing another place where one can amuse himself. I am sure you have heard me speak of M. Blondin who crossed the Niagara. He is here.*

Despite the impression of Cincinnati cosmopolitanism that Eugene Farny tried to convey to his friend in Warren, Cincinnati was still a frontier town. Cows and pigs and chickens roamed the streets. Nearly everyone had his own vegetable garden.

Once in Cincinnati, Charles Farny went into the plaster-molding business with, as it turned out, an unscrupulous partner, and all he was able to save from the resulting financial debacle a few years later was the house on McMicken Street. He leased the ground floor for use as a candy factory. The Farny family lived on the second floor, and the third and fourth floors were leased to others for living quarters.

Leonie, in her late teens when the family moved to Cincinnati, went to work at Atkins' Store, a fashionable dry goods establishment, for six dollars a week, a high wage for a woman at the time. In addition to her work as a sales clerk, here she learned to do filet work in net and silk. Leonie's position at the Atkins' Store was one of the brighter phases of the Farny family's early years in Cincinnati. Her brother Eugene was diagnosed with tuberculosis and died on April 8, 1861. Their father, Charles, was heartbroken at the loss of his son and died two years later on December 19, 1863, at age fifty-three, only ten years after he brought his family to America. Just a week after her father died, Leonie was stricken with typhoid fever but fortunately recovered after a few weeks.

After Leonie's recovery, life of the Farny family on McMicken Street finally brightened. Marguerite and Henri went to school in the thirteenth district, two blocks away, studying using McGuffey's *Eclectic Readers* and Ray's *Practical Arithmetic*. Although Jeannette Farny still did not attend any church, her remaining three children did. Leonie attended a Lutheran church on Sixth Street where the Reverend August Kroell was the pastor; Henri went to a Methodist Sunday school with a friend; and Marguerite went to a Sunday school in a church that she described as the one with the "gold hand pointing up on the steeple," most likely St. Matthews German Evangelical Church at Elm and Liberty Streets. The steeple with the gold hand pointing upward can today be seen atop Philippus United Church of Christ, located on the northwest corner of West McMicken and Ohio Avenues in the Over-the-Rhine neighborhood.

# 4

# THE MARRIAGE OF RUDOLPH AND LEONIE

In the time between Leonie's illness from typhoid and her marriage to Rudolph Wurlitzer, "the little French girl" (as she was called by customers at Atkins' Store) was extremely popular. There were five or six other young men courting her at the time she accepted Rudolph Wurlitzer's proposal of marriage. For that reason, the wedding was a quiet affair on September 19, 1868.

Rudolph Wurlitzer had known Leonie for some time. As an established businessman, he owned a horse and buggy. During one of his frequent recreational drives around town, he noticed an attractive girl on the second-floor balcony of a house on McMicken Street. He drove by the Farny home more and more often on Sunday afternoons and eventually found a friend who knew this attractive girl and thus obtained an introduction. Both had come to America in the same year, 1853. Both came because of rebellion: Rudolph in rebellion against what he considered his father's unreasonable decision of inheritance, Leonie because of her father's rebellion against the religious and political situations in Alsace. Both had high ideals and high moral standards. Both of them were cultured and interested in the finer things in life.

Sylvia, the eldest child of the family, was born about a year after the marriage in their first home on Smith Street on September 21, 1869. The second child was a boy, Howard Eugene, born on September 5, 1871, at 60 Franklin Street. Rudolph Henry was born two years later on December 12, 1873. Next was a daughter, Leonie Jeannette, named after her mother, also

Rudolph Wurlitzer and Leonie Farny at the time of their wedding. *Courtesy of North Tonawanda History Museum.*

born after an interval of about two years, on December 14, 1875. Again in about two years, on November 26, 1877, Percy was born, but unfortunately, he did not survive infancy, dying on July 25, 1878. The youngest of the family was Farny Reginald Wurlitzer, born December 7, 1883.

The family was close knit, but in the German tradition, the father and mother's relationship, while close and affectionate, was reserved and undemonstrative. This is shown in a letter that Rudolph wrote to his wife from Sonneberg, Germany, on April 15, 1870, during one of his occasional trips to his homeland in search of musical instruments.

Rudolph addressed his wife with the affectionate diminutive "Dearest Linchen" but signed himself, rather austerely, "Yours faithfully, R. Wurlitzer." Rudolph's personality is further revealed by the letter itself, one of the few papers preserved from those early days:

> *Since I wrote you last from Nurnberg, I went to Markneukirchen & arrived there last Saturday night, received there one letter of the 14th March waiting for me & the other of the 24th next day. I was very glad to hear from you*

The Wurlitzer home beginning in 1871 at 60 Franklin Street, across from the old Woodward High School. In 1895, Cincinnati changed its address numbering system, renumbering this address to 320. In 1907, Woodward Street, a block to the south, was renamed East Thirteenth Street, and Franklin Street took the name Woodward Street. In 1955, the whole block including the street that contained 320 Woodward Street was eliminated for expansion of Woodward High School's playground. *Courtesy of William E. Griess Jr.*

*& to know that you are all well. I received there the heartiest welcome by everybody, Saturday night when I come, my sister sent word to our father in Schöneck, of my arrival & next day he came with 3 more that I knew, father stayed till Tuesday morning & then went home again, of course I had to promise that I soon would come over & make a good stay as Schöneck expects to see me—(of course such a big man as I am is a wonder, but then these people are that way), they feel as if I belong to them because I was born there, for instance a man of about 54 years that came over with my father, by the name of Carl Ruttel gave me a kiss for welcome & he is not at all related to me—well on Sunday of course I had to talk most all day, On Monday & Tuesday also whenever I was home but I also attended some business and left again Wednesday morning at 3½ o'clock for Lichtenfels, Bavaria, where I arrived in the afternoon, attended to my business & left the next morning for Neustadt & last night for here where I arrived about 9*

*o'clock, but I was too tired to write & now 5 in the morning I cannot spend much time neither with it as I have to be very careful how I spend it, having so much to do yet & travelling here is slow & very uncomfortable at nights.*

*Whether I can come home for the Sangerfest I cannot tell yet, but can likely about 1ˢᵗ of May & will let you know soon as I can—*

*Your picture & Sylvias is admired a good deal by all I have shown it to—I forgot—in Nurnberg I have seen you and Sylvia in life size through an instrument & a light which reflects the picture on the wall—I have bought some of these instruments.*

*I was very glad Sylvia is getting teeth easy & hope she will get them all that way.*

*If you can do without buying any more furniture, I wish you would wait until I come home as we might then buy a whole new set for the parlor. I have also seen new styles of furniture with some of my friends but think it won't come too high to import to America.*

*April 16. I had to quit yesterday as the wagon was ready that I ordered to take me to some factories in the woods some miles from here. I rode over some mountains with considerable snow & ice & return home about 8 o'clock PM and after supper went to bed as I was tired—I don't know how it is but ever since I am in Europe I awake early in the morning most always 6 sometimes sooner, this morning at 5 & as I could not sleep anymore, got up at about 5½ o'clock & finished your letter. So you see I am trying my best to be a good boy.*

*In Leipsig I expect to hear from you again.*

In this letter, we see a prosperous and successful young family man on one of his frequent business trips to Europe. He graciously endures, somewhat tongue-in-cheek, the attentions and adulation of family and friends, some of whom he had scarcely known in the old days in Schöneck. And importantly, he shows that he is fully reconciled with his father.

This letter also reveals Rudolph's pride in his family in the showing of the picture of his "Linchen" and baby Sylvia and of his undemonstrative but deep affection for his young wife in getting up at five-thirty in the morning to finish a letter to her. He shows his interest in their home, especially in his reference to the possibility of importing some furniture. There is also a hint of the strenuous buying program he has set for himself—the hard journeys and long days of his buying trip.

Just after his return from his European trip, Rudolph bought the large brick house on Franklin Street. Rudolph and Leonie lived in the house

*Left*: Rudolph Wurlitzer, 1831–1914. *Lithograph by Krebs Lith. Co. Courtesy of William E. Griess Jr.*

*Right*: Leonie Farny Wurlitzer, 1842–1931. *Photograph by J.&W. Vincent. Courtesy of William E. Griess Jr.*

until 1901, at which time they moved to their final home, the Auburndale Apartments in Mount Auburn.

Although Rudolph was fond of fine horses and carriages, there was never any carriage house on the property. He was one of the first in Cincinnati to buy an automobile—first a Winton and then a Franklin. He played billiards every Saturday night at his club, the Musik Verein, and was usually home by ten o'clock.

Leonie typically entertained by having women in for the afternoon for coffee and pastries. With a large family, she had household help with a cook, an upstairs maid and a laundress. As soon as the daughters were old enough, each prepared the family meals one day a week. Leonie's mother, Jeannette, and her sister, Leonie's aunt Josephine, who had never married, lived with the family most of the time in their old age.

The meals were served punctually and were prepared from recipes from both sides of the family, old Alsatian recipes used almost daily, as well as some from the German Wurlitzer side and, of course, some distinctly American dishes. The family published a cookbook of these recipes in 1925 (see Bibliography). In addition to recipes, the book includes a section devoted to home remedies. Many of these recipes appeared in the Wurlitzer Centennial

The Wurlitzer and Farny women in a photo that appeared in the company's centennial cookbook. Rudolph's wife, Leonie, is at top right; her sister, Marguerite Farny Strobel, is next to her, top left. Their mother Jeannette Farny is directly in front of Leonie; Jeannette's sister, Josephine Weigand, is on Jeannette's right. Leonie's daughters Leonie Wurlitzer Eilers and Sylvia Wurlitzer (Weinberg) Farny are at far left and far right, respectively. *From* A Book of Recipes Covering Three Generations of the Wurlitzer Family and the Wives of Present Business Associates.

Cook Book in 1956, along with additional, more modern recipes submitted by wives of the company's business associates.

Sylvia, Howard, Rudolph H. and Leonie were all brought up to speak French and German as well as English. But by the time Farny came along, English had become the dominant language in the household. When Farny went to Germany in 1901, he realized that he knew very little German. And he had to go to some lengths to master his French language skills while he was in Europe.

Young Leonie's aunt Marguerite ran the household in the early years when their mother Leonie accompanied Rudolph on his European buying trips. After Marguerite married and moved to suburban Norwood, Sylvia took over running the household. For several years, Jeannette and Aunt Josephine spent winters with Leonie on Franklin Street and summers with Marguerite in Norwood.

The Wurlitzer business had become very prosperous and was constantly expanding. Rudolph (often with Leonie) would spend several months in

Europe on buying trips every other year or so. Since the sons were still too young to run the business in their father's absence, this fell to Rudolph's younger brother Anton.

Anton came to America during the Civil War. After he arrived in Cincinnati, he worked for his brother Rudolph, but he enlisted on June 10, 1861, in the Ohio Volunteers, Seventh Regiment, and reported at Camp Dennison. He was wounded in the Battle of Winchester in Virginia on March 23, 1862, with a bullet entering his face just above the cheekbone. The bullet was never removed, and after being hospitalized for three months, he was given a medical discharge in Cincinnati on July 10, 1862.

Anton rejoined the business as soon as he was able and was quickly taken into partnership by Rudolph. The business was renamed Rudolph Wurlitzer & Brother, a name that was retained until 1890. The company was among the largest dealers of band instruments in the United States but also distributed German toys, manufactured musical instruments and furnished drums and trumpets for the Union army. Toy distribution was later discontinued in order to focus on musical instruments.

About this time, Anton married Marie Stolle of Charleston, West Virginia, a German girl whom he met while in the army. Anton became an American citizen in the probate court of Hamilton County, Ohio, on October 30, 1868, because of his status as an honorably discharged veteran. He ran the business successfully during Rudolph's extended European buying trips until Rudolph's son Howard was old enough to take the reins.

The first catalogue was a handwritten list, alphabetized and bound in leather for the personal use of Rudolph Wurlitzer. It had a small section under the heading "Music Boxes" and subheadings "Toy," "Tin" and "Horn." These were imported from Germany or Switzerland, and each played from one to four "airs."

The 1879 catalogue listed a variety of reed organs with pin cylinders in which the music was produced by turning a crank. The cylinders would play six or eight tunes, and at least one line of these "organs" was produced by Henry Cashard in Paris. Prices ranged from $15 to $70. The same catalogue showed pipe organs "with crank," including one in mahogany with three cylinders carrying twenty-seven tunes, selling for $200. The "automatic pianist" was listed at $450 with four and a half octaves of automatic fingers, with crank, "and using perforated Music, by which any Piano can be played mechanically." The price included "10 pieces of selected music on perforated card board. Extra music furnished at reasonable prices."

# NINETEENTH EDITION.

## Catalogue and Descriptive Price List

—OF—

# MUSICAL MERCHANDISE AND STRINGS.

# RUDOLPH WURLITZER & BRO.

Importers and Manufacturers.

## No. 115 Main Street, Cincinnati, Ohio.

Copyright Secured.

Rudolph Wurlitzer & Brother's 1880 catalogue offered 215 pages of musical merchandise.

## To the Musical Trade.

WE take great pleasure in placing before our friends and patrons, this, the Nineteenth Edition of our Illustrated Catalogue and Price List.

We have spared neither time, labor, nor expense to make it complete and perfect in every detail, and to give our customers at a distance some idea of the resources of our firm, and of a stock of Musical Merchandise, which, for variety and extent, is second to none in the United States. For more than a quarter of a century our Catalogues have been regularly sent to our patrons, at first in pamphlet form every other year, and since then in ever-increasing size and at shortened intervals, until a large yearly edition, and a book of this size is required to meet the demand of our business.

We shall be pleased to open accounts with new customers, who make their responsibility known to us, or we will ship any Goods C. O. D., with privilege of examination, provided the amount is more than $5.00, and the distance from the city is not too great. Small orders, amounting to less than $5.00, and ALL orders from a great distance, the Pacific States, and Territories, etc., must be invariably accompanied by the cash. To avoid unnecessary correspondence, dealers not known to us, in sending orders, are requested to give the names of houses here, or elsewhere, with whom they deal, as references. All business men will acknowledge the necessity of this rule.

We shall continue, as heretofore, to preserve the high reputation which our Band Instruments have maintained for beauty and finish of workmanship, quality of material, correctness and timbre of tone, and we warrant all instruments bearing our name to be first-class in every respect. None will be allowed to leave the house which have not stood the test of a thorough examination by a competent artist, whom we employ for this purpose. In orders by mail, our labor will be greatly facilitated if this Catalogue is freely consulted, and the numbers of the same quoted. We give prompt and personal attentions to such orders, and with our long business experience, we are confident that we can make satisfactory selections in all cases where selection or discretion is left with us.

To the thousands of our customers in every State and Territory of the Union, in Canada, the West Indies, and Mexico, we take this occasion to acknowledge our obligations for their many favors in the past, and hoping that we shall be deemed worthy of their continued patronage, we are,

Most respectfully yours,

RUDOLPH WURLITZER & BRO.

Preface from the 1880 catalogue.

Fortunately, all three of Rudolph's sons were interested in the business. His brother Anton had no sons and but one daughter. Because no one in his family could continue his active part in the business, at Anton's request, Rudolph purchased his brother's interest in the business in 1898, and Anton retired to his farm at Fair Smith Station, Butler County, Ohio. Here, he died from a stroke on June 17, 1901. His wife, for eighteen

## CATALOGUE
OF
# RUDOLPH WURLITZER & BRO.

### GERMAN ACCORDEONS.

During recent years the sale of Accordeons has immensely increased, and become an important element in the trade of Musical Instruments. Their elegance, their sweetness of tone, their ready facility to play them, and their cheapness, insure them a great future.

We have the greatest demand for first-class goods, and we have used our best endeavors to furnish Accordeons of which materials and workmanship have been selected with the most scrupulous care.

No. 12. Nos. 10, 11, 13 are of the same style and finish.

### WITH ONE SET OF REEDS.

| No. | | | | | | | | | | Each. |
|---|---|---|---|---|---|---|---|---|---|---|
| 10 | 6 German Silver Keys, | | 2 Basses, Imitation Rosewood | | | | | | | $ 80 |
| 11 | 8 | " | " | " | 2 | " | | " | | 1 00 |
| 12 | 10 | " | " | " | 2 | " | | " | | 1 20 |
| 13 | 12 | " | " | " | 2 | " | | " | | 1 50 |

No. 50. Nos. 49 and 51 are of the same style and finish.

### WITH TWO SETS OF REEDS.

| No. | | | | | | | | | | Each. |
|---|---|---|---|---|---|---|---|---|---|---|
| 38 | 10 German Silver Keys, 1 Stop, 2 Basses, Concave Molding, Trumpets, G. S. Corners and Holder, with Silver Pressed Ornaments on top | | | | | | | | | $3 50 |
| 49 | 8 German Silver Keys, 1 Stop, 2 Basses, Concave Molding | | | | | | | | | 2 00 |
| 50 | 10 | " | " | " | 1 | " | 2 | " | " | " | 2 50 |
| 51 | 12 | " | " | " | 1 | " | 2 | " | " | " | . . . 3 00 |

A sample page from the 1880 catalogue.

years a victim of paralysis, had died on November 29, 1898, at about the time of Anton's retirement.

Rudolph's brother-in-law Adolph (Charles) Strobel also was active in the Wurlitzer business in those early days. He was associated with the business until June 1899; he died on August 28, 1906, in New York City.

# 5
# The Artist Henry Farny

While the Wurlitzer side of the family focused on music, Leonie's brother Henri François Farny leaned toward the arts in the form of painting. He became a well-known painter of western people and scenes and signed his name Henry F. Farny.

Henry drew pictures before he could talk, according to his youngest sister, Marguerite. His mother, Jeannette, often amused him by drawing circles on paper, and Henry would add to them, turning the circles into bodies. He had just turned six when the family landed in New York. He amused himself while on the train riding across New York State by sketching people and scenes on a pad of paper. Since paper was scarce in the backwoods Tionesta homestead, indulgent Aunt Josephine let him draw on the plain flat-board walls. When he had filled up a wall, she washed off the pictures, and he would draw again.

Henry was a charmer and a storyteller. In Tionesta, at the age of eight, he and a neighbor boy, David Itell, were sent to do farm chores. His father, Charles, came upon them a little later and found David working hard while Henry sat nearby, spinning enchanting yarns for David in return for which David was doing all the work. Throughout his life, Henry was the center of any group.

After moving to Cincinnati, in 1859, Henry Farny went to Woodward High School but left before graduating in order to go to work to help support the family during the last year of his father's illness and after his death. Before his father's death, Henry took a position in the Goepper malt

Henry F. Farny, 1847–1916. *Photograph by Nancy Ford Cones. Courtesy of William E. Griess Jr.*

business as a bookkeeper. Charles didn't approve of Henry's artistic leanings and sought to get a job for Henry in a more practical field, but Mr. Goepper told Charles that it was not likely that Henry would become a bookkeeper since he spent most of his time drawing pictures on the ledgers instead of doing his work.

Later, he had a job painting decorations on water coolers. He also worked for various engravers and lithographers, including Gibson and Company of Cincinnati, for whom he did Civil War scenes. His first big success was a caricature of Jefferson Davis for which *Harper's Weekly* paid him a bonus of two dollars in addition to his regular stipend of two dollars.

Henry did not stay in Cincinnati long after his father died. His restless ambition sent him to New York City when he was seventeen to work as an artist for *Harper's Weekly*. He became acquainted with a famous American author and portrait painter of the day, Thomas Buchanan Read (1822–1872), whom he may have met in Cincinnati. Read is best known for his stirring poem "Sheridan's Ride." Read left to live in Rome and wrote to Henry in New York, urging him to join him and his wife to further his art education.

So, Henry gave up his work at the magazine and sailed for Italy. Italy and its art treasures broadened Henry's education. He met many artists, notably Henri Regnault, but became saddened and distressed when he realized that his friend Read was a confirmed alcoholic. It was also during his time with the Reads that he learned of the death of his great-aunt Marguerite Farny in Colmar, Alsace. She had sent Christmas boxes and garden seeds to the Farny family during their difficult days near Warren, Pennsylvania. She had bequeathed him a considerable amount of money, and he set out for Alsace to claim it. This bequest enabled Henry to continue his art studies abroad in Paris, Dusseldorf, Munich, Strasbourg and Vienna, studying with Michael Munkacsy and other famous painters of the day but never for long with any one teacher.

While he was studying in Dusseldorf in April, probably 1873, he wrote a rather amusing letter to his sister Leonie, noting the fact that her husband, Rudolph, had just visited him on one of his numerous trips to Europe.

> *A half hour's talk made us better acquainted than scores of letters and photos could have done. We talked almost all night—he only came one day and left the next. Of all the numerous beaux that pursued you of yore, I know none who was one half as manly and earnest as I found him to be, and once more I congratulate you. You must have painted me in rather dark colors for he naively told me he was much better pleased with me than he thought he would be.*

Henry added that he had at last decided to go home to Cincinnati.

> *It has been a tough struggle between ambition and homesickness—between art and my future on one side and home on the other.*

Henry stayed in Europe as long as he could, about three years, taking jobs when he could find them. He returned to Cincinnati by steerage in 1873 and planned to make a living as an artist. Unfortunately, his paintings did not sell, so he turned to work as a commercial artist. He designed posters for John Robinson's Circus and drew cartoons for local newspapers, more illustrations for *Harper's Weekly* and anything else available. The Cincinnati Chamber of Commerce commissioned him to produce a cartoon on the pork packing industry for the Vienna Exposition. Farny delivered the cartoon himself in Vienna and then went to Munich and studied with Professor Diez. In Munich, he first became friends with Cincinnati-area artist Frank Duveneck (1848–1919). He returned to Cincinnati in 1876.

Restless and ambitious but frustrated, Farny still wanted a career as an artist. During the late 1870s and early '80s, he made several trips into the West, and his years of study began to pay off. He had the vision to apply what he learned in design and color to a realistic portrayal of Indian life.

Henry's interest in Indian life is best explained in his own words. In one of a series of articles that the *Cincinnati Enquirer* ran on Sunday, June 24, 1900, under the title, "When They Were Boys," he described his early encounters

*Cincinnati Opera Festival, Scene From the First Act of Lohengrin.* Illustration by Henry Farny for *Harper's Weekly*, February 3, 1883. *From the collection of the Public Library of Cincinnati and Hamilton County.*

with Indians. He speaks of his father running the sawmill on the upper reaches of the Allegheny River and of his early erroneous ideas of Indians, ideas conveyed by the tall tales of lumberjacks whom he grew to know as "accomplished kingpin liars."

*My idea of an Indian was that he was a sort of bloodthirsty human ferret, noiseless and insatiable for gore, and the chief ambition of my life was to learn to swing an axe and become a dead shot with a rifle. Only once had I seen one of these terrible red men during one of the rare visits to Warren, the county seat, with my father. I saw a crowd gathered around a wagon in which sat an Indian, and there lay an enormous dead panther, which he had killed and brought in to claim the fifty dollar reward. But then there were lots of white people about, and my father was with me, and I was not afraid.*

*You can imagine my horror, therefore, when I was chopping kindling wood in the woodshed one bitter cold day to hear a voice at my elbow suddenly say, "Little boy! Little boy!" On looking up, I beheld an Indian who had come in noiselessly. He was a pleasant old man in a fringed hunting shirt and fur cap. A rifle lay in the hollow of his arm, and a hatchet was in his belt.*

*For a moment, I was paralyzed with fear, for I devoutly believed I was about to be made into a meat salad. I then let out a series of such bloodcurdling yells that even the men in the sawmill heard me and came running to see what was up.*

*The Indian was Old Jacob, a famous Seneca hunter. Jacob was half starved, and my father took him in and made him sit down to dinner with us and kept him overnight. The old man became our fast friend, and many a haunch of venison did he bring to pay for that day's hospitality. When he found my father was a Frenchman, he insisted that his people and my father's people were friends farther back than the oldest man in the tribe could remember. He even brought a silver medal the French king had given his ancestors and celebrated the occasion by a song and dance, with the aid of a skillet on which he drummed with his hunting knife.*

*Of course, he and I became great chums. He would take me to his camp, show me how to make moccasins and bows and arrows, and later when hunting parties of his tribe came near us, he would take me to see the shy, unkempt children with beady eyes, and though we could not speak together, we soon learned not to be afraid of each other.*

*Finally, the day came when we left the old Tionestah mill for good and floated down the Allegheny into the Ohio and down the Ohio to Cincinnati on one of my father's rafts, and I never saw Old Jacob again. The memories of those early days in the pine woods and laurel brakes of the Allegheny have always been my pleasantest ones, so that when I grew up to be an artist, it was but natural for me to find a more sympathetic subject for my work in the American Indian than in painting Arabs or Breton or Dutch peasants, as most American painters do.*

The theme fascinated him, and the plight of the western Indians resonated in him. Art lovers sensed the truth and sensitivity in his work and saw him as a master of his craft. The Indian theme made Henry Farny's career. His paintings were in demand, and buyers often waited years for the chance to own a Farny painting.

One of Farny's most significant paintings on the intrusion of the white man into the lands of the Indian, *The Vanguard*, shows a white surveyor looking through a theodolite with a rifle and a shovel nearby. Two guards and a spring wagon with a driver and four horses are about fifty yards away. Off in the distance, two Indians on horseback watch the proceedings. He

*Dance of the Crow Indians* by Henry F. Farny. Illustration from *Harper's Weekly*, December 15, 1883. *From the collection of the Public Library of Cincinnati and Hamilton County.*

was also accomplished in portraiture. In his portrait *Tah-Tonkah-Iotaque, the Uncpapa Sioux*, he distilled all of the bitterness, distrust, suspicion and hatred of the Plains Indian for the intruding white man. In his drawings for popular magazines of the day, he also showed that he was a master of satire. This is demonstrated in his image *Dance of the Crow Indians* that appeared in *Harper's Weekly*.

The caption he wrote tells the story: "The lurid light of the campfires, deafening drum beats, jingling bells of the dancers, and weird monotonous chant of the singers were echoed by the whistle of the locomotives as the excursion trains successively drew up." There was sharp contrast in the scene, dancing Indians surrounded by wide-eyed excursionists and the lighted windows of the railroad train showing in the distance. When writing about this image in his book *Portrait of the Old West*, Harold McCracken noted, "The Old West had become a side show and the Indian dance a sham."

Henry Farny and President Theodore Roosevelt became friends through contacts made in the West. Roosevelt recognized what Farny was trying to portray and told him, "The nation owes you a great debt. It does not realize it now, but it will someday. You are preserving for future generations phases of American history that are rapidly passing away." In 1943, twenty-seven years after Farny's death, the Cincinnati Art Museum mounted an exhibition of 150 of his paintings under the title "Henry F. Farny and the American Indian." Newspapers noted the exhibition with great interest.

"He painted many subjects," the critic for the *Cincinnati Times-Star* wrote,

> *but his pictures of Indian life in the American West, near the close of the last century, were his outstanding works. With a great eye for detail, an intensity of feeling and superb craftsmanship, he captured the tragedy of the Red Man, his romance and the poetry and atmosphere of his surroundings, and put them on canvas. Henry Farny is at last coming into his own as an artist without superior in a field which, neglected though it was, offered limitless possibilities.*

Most of the paintings for the exhibition were loaned by private collectors, many of whom were Cincinnatians.

In July 1947, on the 100th anniversary of Henry's birth in Ribeauvillé, the Cincinnati Art Museum held another exhibition of his work as a centennial observance in his honor. Mary L. Alexander, writing in the *Cincinnati Enquirer* at the time, referred to Henry Farny as "a most popular painter. He couldn't paint his Indian pictures fast enough to please the public. Only those most favored received his canvases. It is widely known fact that Farny would start a picture for one person, but before he had finished it, the demand was so great that another friend probably would receive the original order." Of Henry Farny the man, Alexander wrote, "Farny was as delightful a companion as he was a painter. He had that charming quality of storytelling, which, when expressed in his paintings, preserved for future generations the romantic history of our Western Indians."

Farny was included in the party of Washington, D.C. and foreign notables to witness the driving of the last spike in the transcontinental railroad in the fall of 1883. One of the more remarkable of Farny's paintings is *The Song of the Talking Wire*, now in Cincinnati's Taft Museum. McCracken noted, "There is mingled sadness and bitterness on the face of a lonely brave, still wearing the buffalo robe of his father but reduced to hunting the lowly deer with the white man's gun, while he stops on his way home to contemplate the mysterious humming of the white man's 'talking wire'—a symbol of the red man's destruction."

Henry Farny's illustrations for the McGuffey *Readers* helped to revolutionize schoolbook publishing. Up until that time, most illustrations had been stiff and unreal. Of the three hundred illustrations in the nine volumes published by McGuffey, Farny did seventy-six. He is the only

Factory mark logo designed by Henry Farny for Rookwood Pottery representing a kiln with two rooks. Rookwood used this design from 1880 to 1882, printed in black beneath the glaze. *From* Rookwood VIII & Keramics 1998 *(auction catalogue).*

artist represented in all nine volumes. Later, he was hired as the first artist at Maria Longworth Nichols Storer's Rookwood Pottery Company and designed a logo for the business.

Among Farny's friends were such notables as Mark Twain, George W. Cable, Robert Louis Stevenson, Swedish artist Anders Zorn, General Nelson A. Miles and Sitting Bull. Farny served as art editor for Lafcadio Hearn's humorous weekly that survived only nine issues, *Ye Giglampz.* While he was studying in Paris, he developed a lifelong friendship with actress Sarah Bernhardt. Years later, she was in Cincinnati on a theatrical engagement and visited Farny's studio on Pike Street. She viewed Cincinnati as a horrible place and did her best to persuade Farny to return to Paris with her. Of course, he ignored her advice.

Henry Farny had an unusual personal life. He traveled extensively in Europe and the American West. He learned two Indian languages and was adopted by the Senecas, the Sioux, the Blackfeet and the Zuni.

His early romances were failures. He was very attractive to both men and women but was regarded as a poor marriage risk. He was careless with money and was once chided by the president of the Central National Bank of Cincinnati, who said to him, "Henry, your signature at the bottom of a painting commands great respect, but your signature on the bottom of a check on this bank, when you have no funds, commands none."

Henry eventually did find someone late in life. While living in Covington, Kentucky, he was often visited by nieces and nephews. One of the children who visited along with the nieces and nephews was Ann Ray, of whom he

This 1906 group photo shows Henry Farny (second from left in back row) and his young wife, Ann Ray Farny (second from left in second row). Others in the photo, from left to right, are: *front row*: Valeska Helene Wurlitzer, Luise Henriette Wurlitzer, Janet Wurlitzer, Marianne Leonie Wurlitzer, Rembert Rudolph Wurlitzer, Raimund Billing Wurlitzer; *second row*: Henriette Billing (Howard Wurlitzer's mother-in-law), Ann Ray Farny, Helene Billing Wurlitzer, Rudolph Wurlitzer, Leonie Farny Wurlitzer and Marie Richard Wurlitzer, holding her daughter Natalie Richard Wurlitzer; *back row*: Howard Wurlitzer, Henry Farny, Ilsa Billing Bering (Henriette Billing's sister); S. George Weinberg (later Farny), Herta Lampe (possibly a nurse for Rudolph), Rudolph Henry Wurlitzer and Farny Reginald Wurlitzer. *Courtesy of William E. Griess Jr.*

became particularly fond. Ann's father was ill, and her family was down on its luck. Farny paid to send Ann to a girls' school in Louisville, from which she graduated in 1906 at the age of nineteen. They were married later that year in Jamestown, New York. Farny was then fifty-nine. Their only child was Daniel Henry Farny, born in Cincinnati on February 20, 1908.

Henry F. Farny died on December 23, 1916. With his passing, Cincinnati lost a major figure in the art world, an extroverted artist who kept a large cluttered studio across from the Fourth Street Wurlitzer Store and a man whose Philippine cigars and young wife gave a kind of glamour to his free-and-easy way of life.

# 6
# THE SECOND GENERATION

The five children of Rudolph and Leonie Wurlitzer developed the family music business very successfully, probably beyond their father's wildest dreams. They enriched Cincinnati and beyond through their appreciation and understanding of the music industry and musical arts.

All five inherited the traits of courage, initiative and aggressiveness from their parents. Sylvia and Rudolph Henry each had a lifelong interest in music—Sylvia in piano and Rudolph H. in violin. Howard was an astute businessman, ambitious and aggressive. While he was head of the Wurlitzer Company, he experienced the handicaps of ill health and pain and persistent discouragement, yet he continued to grow the business. Like their mother, Leonie and Sylvia were both excellent household managers and hostesses.

Farny R. Wurlitzer, the youngest son, provided a kind of balance and stability through the business activities of the second generation. He had a calming personality and was able to smooth ruffled feathers and bring about a satisfactory solution to problems. Yet he was also adept in business, eventually running the large Wurlitzer factory established in North Tonawanda, New York. It may have been his relative detachment from the main base of operations in Cincinnati that allowed him to play the peacemaker when necessary.

Rudolph Wurlitzer and his successful business as drawn in caricature by E.A. Bushnell of the Newspaper Cartoonists Association of Cincinnati in 1905. *Courtesy of Archives and Rare Books Library, University of Cincinnati.*

Rudolph and Leonie's fortieth wedding anniversary, 1908. *Front row, left to right*: Fritz Eilers, Farny Eilers, Marguerite Eilers, Eugene Weinberg, Rembert Wurlitzer, Louise Wurlitzer, Valeska Wurlitzer, Marianne Wurlitzer and Janet Wurlitzer. *Second row, left to right*: Raimund Wurlitzer, Helene Wurlitzer, Natalie Wurlitzer (in lap), Leonie Wurlitzer Eilers, Rudolph Wurlitzer, Leonie Farny Wurlitzer, Alice Weinberg, Sylvia Wurlitzer Weinberg, Marie Richard Wurlitzer and Cyril Weinberg. *Third row, left to right*: Karl Eilers, Howard Wurlitzer, Farny Wurlitzer and Rudolph H. Wurlitzer. (The George Weinberg family changed their surname to Farny in 1919.) *Courtesy of William E. Griess Jr.*

# *Sylvia Farny Wurlitzer (Weinberg) Farny*

Destined to live an eventful life, Sylvia, the first child of Rudolph and Leonie Wurlitzer, was born in their home on Smith Street, Cincinnati, on September 21, 1869. She showed an interest in music early in life. She attended Cincinnati public schools and, later, Madame Freddin's private school. She studied piano under various Cincinnati teachers, including a Miss Sparmann. She also studied at the University of Cincinnati.

In 1892, when Sylvia was twenty-three years old and her brother Rudolph H. was about nineteen, they traveled to Berlin accompanied by their great-aunt Josephine as chaperone. Sylvia studied piano, and her brother studied violin. During this trip, Sylvia met Semen George Weinberg, a Russian citizen and a Cossack officer in the Russian army. Weinberg was about twenty and was also studying in Berlin. Sylvia and her brother returned to Cincinnati after about a year, along with their aunt. Weinberg completed his studies and his service in the Russian army three years later.

Rudolph Henry Wurlitzer and his elder sister, Sylvia, about 1892. *Courtesy of William E. Griess Jr.*

After returning to Cincinnati, Sylvia gave piano lessons and continued her studies in music, and apparently, she also kept up a correspondence with Weinberg. As soon as he was free to leave Russia in 1895, Weinberg traveled to Cincinnati. However, shortly before his arrival, Sylvia had left the city on an extended trip to the West Coast with Mrs. Henrietta Billing and others. Weinberg waited in Cincinnati for her for several weeks and in the meantime became fond of Sylvia's younger sister Leonie. But in the end, he proposed marriage to Sylvia, and she accepted. They were married in Cincinnati on February 19, 1896.

George Weinberg became a manufacturers' representative for American products in Russia. He was a charming salesman who made friends easily, and he had been trained as an engineer. He became the representative for several American firms in Russia, including the George Worthington Company, the Laidlaw-Dunn-Gordon Company, the Starrett Company, the Ault and Wilborg Company, the Cleveland Twist Drill Company and others. Assured of a steady income in his native land, George Weinberg and his bride left immediately after the ceremony for Europe on the MS *St. Paul.*

It was a leisurely honeymoon, and the couple eventually settled in St. Petersburg. During their travel to Russia, they paused for days at a time in various cities so George could make business calls. Between March and June, they were in Berlin (where George's sister and her husband lived),

S. George Weinberg, Sylvia Wurlitzer's husband. In 1919, he changed his surname, and that of his wife and children, to Farny. *Courtesy of William E. Griess Jr.*

Paris, Strasbourg and Warsaw, arriving in Moscow by late May. They spent June and July in St. Petersburg. In August, they were welcomed into the Weinberg family home at Rostov-on-Don. They returned to St. Petersburg in October.

They settled down to live in St. Petersburg, where George opened offices as a dealer in American products, particularly machinery. They traveled back to Cincinnati for the birth of their first son, Eugene Rudolph, on April 14, 1897; he died in March 1987. George returned to St. Petersburg a few weeks later, but Sylvia stayed in Cincinnati for several more months. George returned to America in 1899 to study at the Michigan Mining School in Houghton. He graduated as a mining engineer in 1901 and established himself as an engineering consultant.

George and Sylvia had two more children: Cyril was born in Teriojoki, then a part of Finland, on June 1, 1903; he died on September 26, 1990. Alice Leonie was born in St. Petersburg on October 14, 1905; she died on March 6, 1998. Their parents were determined to raise all three of their children as Americans.

Their life in Russia was pleasant, with entertaining and frequent visits from George Weinberg's Rostov relatives as well as members of the Wurlitzer family and Cincinnati friends. They were a part of the pleasant St. Petersburg society of the time with its lengthy celebrations that marked the crowning of the ill-fated Nicholas II. They had three servants in their apartment.

Sylvia's mother and Aunt Marguerite were visiting them in St. Petersburg in 1914 when World War I began. Eugene, Sylvia's first son, was about to enter Harvard College, and he accompanied his grandmother and great-aunt to America in the fall of that year, leaving Russia through the Scandinavian countries and England, landing in Montreal and proceeding to Cincinnati.

Because of Russian duties on American goods, George Weinberg found it increasingly difficult to represent American exporters. He relied on his work as a consulting engineer for mining companies in Russia and China. He built the first electrolytic plant for the Bogoslov Mining Company for the extraction of copper. He engineered a bridge over the River Don and designed the waterworks system of the city of Nicolaef and an incinerator plant for St. Petersburg. He also served as consulting engineer for the Turkish government to plan a national highway system.

With the Russian Revolution looming on the horizon, Weinberg recognized it as the end of their life in his native land. In 1916, Sylvia and the two younger children escaped through Sweden, Norway and Scotland to America. Months later, her husband made his way east along the Trans-Siberian Railway and sailed for America from Vladivostok. He was in Japan on his way to America in January 1917. The Russian Revolution began a few months later.

Although he had been able to transfer some funds to America, George left his family behind, as well as prized possessions such as the Steinway grand piano that his father-in-law Rudolph Wurlitzer shipped from America to Sylvia as a gift.

Now a refugee, George Weinberg joined his wife and children in America with the realization that the old life in Russia was ended and began to create a new life. He took an examination and was assigned the rank of major in the United States Army Corps of Engineers in April 1917. He traveled to Washington to meet with President Wilson, since he believed that his knowledge of Russia might be useful to the American government. Wilson ordered Major Weinberg to travel to Russia to report on conditions, so he left early in May, arriving in St. Petersburg late in the month. He spent the summer there with the exception of short periods at his summer home in Finland, which he later sold. He witnessed much of the street fighting and riots in St. Petersburg and saw the beginning and the end of the Kornilov counterrevolution.

That summer, President Wilson also sent an official mission to Russia headed by Elihu Root (1845–1937), former United States secretary of war. Root's party returned to America with a report praising Russian minister of war Alexander Kerensky and assuring the president that Russia would stay in the war and could be counted upon. Major Weinberg submitted his report with exactly the opposite opinion, which unfortunately was ignored by Wilson.

Immediately on his return to the United States, Major Weinberg was assigned to the Thirtieth Engineers, stationed at Fort Myers, Virginia, a regiment made up almost completely of chemical engineers. The regiment was to sail for France on December 25, 1917. It had no colonel, and on the day before sailing, the lieutenant colonel became ill, so command fell to Major Weinberg.

When peace finally arrived, George Weinberg came to the conclusion that his surname would be a handicap in view of what had happened in Russia. He faced the fact that he would spend the rest of his life in America. For those reasons and on the urging of Sylvia, in the summer of 1919, he legally changed his surname, and that of his family, to Farny. The Farny name was chosen out of the high regard George held for the Farnys, particularly Henry Farny, the painter.

George Farny could speak English, French, German and Russian fluently, as well as some Italian. He became active in the planning of roads and parks to meet the needs created by increased use of the automobile. For a time, he was vice-president of the National Highways Association and chairman of the National County Roads Planning Association. There is today Farny State Park of nearly five thousand acres in Morris County, New Jersey. It was named in his honor in recognition and appreciation of his efforts in the development of the state's highways and park areas.

In 1917, Major George and Sylvia Wurlitzer Farny purchased the six-hundred-acre Craftsman Farms, also in Morris County, at a bankruptcy sale. The property had been the home of Gustav Stickley, a major figure in Craftsman furniture design. The Farny family maintained the farm in Stickley's tradition, adapting some interior features for modern family life. They also built several guest cottages for rental and renamed the property Pigeon Hill Club Community. Their son Cyril Farny and his wife, Phyllis Holt (whom he married in 1928), as well as their four children, occupied the property until the late 1980s. When the property was threatened with development for fifty-two town houses, the Township of Parsippany-Troy Hills, with the encouragement of community groups and others interested in the importance of the site, obtained the property through eminent domain. Known once again as Craftsman Farms, this National Historic Landmark site now houses a museum of Stickley's work.

George Farny died on September 1, 1941, at the age of sixty-nine, thirteen days after suffering a heart attack while attending the funeral of his brother-in-law Karl Eilers at Sea Cliff, Long Island. Family and friends were puzzled when Sylvia did not seem to show grief. Her explanation was simple and sincere. "When George and I were married more than forty-five years ago, I never dreamed that we would have so many happy years together.

The main house at Craftsman Farms, originally the home of Gustav Stickley, the creator of Craftsman furniture and a visionary of the Arts and Crafts movement. George and Sylvia Farny moved here in 1917. Today, it is a museum dedicated to Stickley. *Photo by Ray Stubblebine, courtesy of the Craftsman Farms Foundation, Inc., Parsippany, New Jersey.*

Why should I be sad now?" A Unitarian in her early years, after the move to New Jersey, Sylvia became an Episcopalian. In her later years, she lived in a remodeled cottage on the Pigeon Hill estate and died there on March 10, 1952.

## *Howard Eugene Wurlitzer*

Howard Eugene Wurlitzer was the second child and eldest son of Rudolph and Leonie Wurlitzer. He was born on September 5, 1871, in Cincinnati.

Howard attended the public schools in Cincinnati but left after three years at Woodward High School because he was needed in the family business. Beginning at age seventeen, he quickly learned the ropes from his father and from George Metzel, who was with the company for thirty years.

In 1890, when he was twenty, his parents took him on a buying trip to Europe as a sort of postgraduate course in business education. Howard met many of the suppliers in Germany, France and Switzerland who had sold musical instruments to Rudolph Wurlitzer for many years. They sailed in early April on the SS *Trave* of the North German Lloyd Line.

Howard wrote to his sister from Markneukirchen on May 27, 1890, describing the spectacle that he saw in Berlin: a review of troops by the Kaiser. From their seats in the grandstand, he described the scene. Afterward, Howard got an opportunity to take a photo of the emperor, but he remarked to Sylvia that the Kaiser "looked very tired and hot" and "the people didn't hurrah very much and weren't enthusiastic at all." Of Berlin itself, Howard remarked that he had "expected more. Everything goes so confoundedly slow and *gemütlich*. I always felt like I wanted to push the people along or put some electricity into them. There isn't the rush and activity that there is in a large American city."

Howard married Helene Valeska Billing of Salt Lake City, the daughter of a successful mining engineer active in the copper mining and smelting business, a man who was closely associated with Anton Eilers, whose son was later to marry Howard's younger sister, Leonie. The marriage took place in Cincinnati on November 5, 1895.

Howard and Helene had three children. The eldest child was Raimund Billing Wurlitzer, born on November 24, 1896, in Cincinnati and died in 1986. He was married on December 30, 1920, at Oconomowoc, Wisconsin, to Pauline Tekla Pabst. The second child was Luise Henriette, who was born on October 20, 1898, and died on February 14, 1924. The third was Valeska Helene, born on December 28, 1900, in Cincinnati. She married August Thoman of Covington, Kentucky, on August 28, 1924; she died on July 26, 1940.

Howard and his wife actively supported Cincinnati's musical life. Helene served on the board of the College of Music of Cincinnati and, among other things, conceived and financed the idea of a radio and television department at the college for the study and application of this medium for musical expression. In 1955, the college bestowed upon her an honorary doctorate. After her husband's death, Helene established the Helene Wurlitzer Foundation of New Mexico to support the arts in Taos, New Mexico, where she lived.

During the next twenty-five years, Howard was a major factor in the success of the business. He had a memory for detail and could quickly size up people. He was impatient with inefficiency and carelessness. True or not, the story is told that if he did not like the way an employee kept his desk, that employee might come to the office some morning and find the contents of all the drawers dumped on top of the desk. From that he could start afresh. He had the knack of making loyal friends; at the same time, there were others who hated him intensely. There was very little in between.

Beginning around the turn of the century, his father Rudolph gradually withdrew from active participation in the business. Ailing for many months before he died on January 14, 1914, Rudolph was confined to the family apartment at the Auburndale Apartments under nursing care.

The year 1914 was an evil one for the Wurlitzers. Not only did the family lose its head and the founder of the business, but Howard was also stricken with appendicitis. There was an operation, but he acquired a streptococcus infection and was seriously ill. Dr. Edward C. Rosenow from Chicago treated him and developed a serum that he administered. Howard improved

Howard Eugene Wurlitzer. *Photograph by Rawleigh. Courtesy of William E. Griess Jr.*

somewhat, but from the time of the operation until he died on October 30, 1928, he was never a well man. However, he persisted in his work with the business, running it very successfully. After many futile and discouraging attempts to find relief, in 1921, Dr. George Washington Crile of Cleveland diagnosed the ailment as Banti's disease. At one point, Howard was so ill that he traveled to the Mayo Clinic in Rochester, Minnesota, for treatment, to little effect. Later, after hearing of a physician in Germany who might help him, at considerable expense and enormous physical effort, he made the trip to Germany. The results were partially successful and, from his viewpoint, well worth the effort, although he was still handicapped by the disease.

During the early years in business, Howard regularly visited with his uncle Henry Farny, whose studio was across the street from the Rudolph Wurlitzer Company Building, and the two often had lunch together.

During the better days before 1914, Howard and Helene often spent their vacations in Germany. Because of their complex family and business connections in Germany, both of them were definitely pro-German before America entered World War I. After the United States entered the war, the couple was unswervingly loyal to the United States.

The Wurlitzer family as a whole was very much divided in its sympathies during World War I. Leonie, the mother of Howard and Rudolph, was a native of Alsace and naturally sympathized with the French. It was inevitable that she was distressed over the German sympathies of her two elder sons.

On the other hand, Sylvia naturally had strong ties with Russia. She certainly was not pro-German, noting in a letter to her mother on April 5, 1916, "I was very sorry to hear that you and the boys have again excited each other about the war. It is very silly for the boys to say that we"—meaning Sylvia and her husband—"are on their side, for it seems to me it goes without saying, that we cannot possibly be pro-German, because we ourselves have lost so heavily and will continue to lose still more heavily, if the Germans should win."

When they were first married, Howard and Helene built a home near that of Mrs. Billing. Around 1914, Howard built a more elaborate house overlooking the Ohio River, with an apartment for his mother-in-law on the third floor. The house at Number 6 Beechcrest Lane was named "Schoeneck" (Beautiful Corner) for the Saxon village where Howard's father had been born. After the painter Uncle Henry Farny had been married for a few years, he bought a home across the street from Howard because of his affection for his nephew.

Howard Wurlitzer was the person responsible for getting the Rudolph Wurlitzer Company into the coin-operated piano and orchestrion business, and as a result of his leadership, the Wurlitzer Company prospered. Howard was first employed full time by the partnership of Rudolph Wurlitzer & Brother in 1889. He was elected to the board of directors of the newly incorporated Rudolph Wurlitzer Company on March 29, 1890, and became vice-president of the company on April 25, 1898. On July 23, 1912, he was elected president of the company and held that position until he became chairman of the board on July 11, 1927. However, his long-lasting leadership and influence was to come to an unexpected and rather abrupt end.

The *Music Trades Review* of May 12, 1928, had an article with the headline: "Rudolph H. and Farny R. Wurlitzer to Take Over Interests of Howard E. Wurlitzer and Family in the Rudolph Wurlitzer Co."

*CINCINNATI, O., May 7.—From the headquarters of the Rudolph Wurlitzer Co. this week comes the announcement that Rudolph H. Wurlitzer and Farny R. Wurlitzer have arranged to purchase the interests of Howard E. Wurlitzer and his immediate family in the Rudolph Wurlitzer Co. Howard E. Wurlitzer is retiring from active participation in the business of the company. There will be no change in the management of the business.*

Also in 1928, sister Leonie's stock interests were bought out by the Wurlitzer Company, reportedly as a result of dissension among family members. It is probably no coincidence that this buyout corresponds with the abrupt departure of Howard E. Wurlitzer (officially noted as his retirement) and suggests that the Wurlitzer family had some deeply entrenched rivalries.

Another item appeared in the November 3, 1928 issue of *Presto Music Times* with this headline: "HOWARD WURLITZER DIES IN NEW YORK. Former Chairman of the Board of the Rudolph Wurlitzer Company Passes Away at 1 a.m. Tuesday at the Ritz Hotel After One Week's Illness." The obituary continues,

*Howard E. Wurlitzer, aged 57 years, former chairman of the Board of the Rudolph Wurlitzer Company, manufacturers of pianos, harps, organs and coin-operated instruments, died at 1 a.m. Tuesday of this week at the Ritz Hotel, New York, of influenza. Mr. Wurlitzer, whose home was in Cincinnati, had gone east to visit his mother on her recent birthday, and he was ill only a week. He had had some hemorrhages. The funeral was held at Cincinnati on Friday, and all the Wurlitzer offices in the various cities were closed on that day…Mr. Wurlitzer left Cincinnati on October 26 to go to Morristown, N.J., to attend the celebration of the birthday of his mother, Mrs. Leonie F. Wurlitzer, at the home of her daughter, Mrs. Sylvia, Morristown. After the celebration Mr. Wurlitzer became ill and died two days later.*

## Rudolph Henry Wurlitzer

Rudolph Henry Wurlitzer, the second son and third child of Rudolph and Leonie Wurlitzer, was born on December 30, 1873, in Cincinnati, about two years after Howard. The two were quite different in temperament. Howard matured into a quick, aggressive, hardheaded businessman. Rudolph was more interested in cultural things, especially music, and was something of a mystic.

Like Howard, Rudolph H. attended Cincinnati public schools and Woodward High School, but unlike Howard, his father permitted him to continue until he graduated. After graduation from Woodward, Rudolph

*Left*: Rudolph Henry Wurlitzer. *Photograph by Elite Studio. Courtesy of William E. Griess Jr.*

*Below*: The Wurlitzer family gathered in the parlor for an evening's entertainment. *Courtesy of Regional History Center, Northern Illinois University.*

H. went to Berlin with his sister Sylvia for further study. He studied at the University of Berlin, as well as privately with Emanuel Wirth (1842–1923) of the famous Joachim Quartet. In Berlin, Rudolph H. began to build his knowledge of the violin and its manufacture that made him an expert on the instrument later in life.

While at the University of Berlin, he studied the history of musical instruments under Oscar Fleischer. He listened to lectures by Helmholtz and Kundt on acoustics and physics and Spitta on the history of music. He was able to spend two afternoons a week in the shop of August Riechers (1836–1893), a violin maker, through whom he gained a basic knowledge of violins, violin making and the famous makers. Riechers had learned his trade under Carl Friedrich Fickers in Markneukirchen and also worked under Ludwig Bausch, a violin bow specialist. Riechers not only repaired violins but also made them following the Stradivarius pattern.

Returning to Cincinnati, Rudolph H. immediately joined the family business. He also found time to pursue his interest in the violin, sponsoring concerts in Cincinnati in 1895 and 1896.

Rudolph H. married Marie Richard of Cincinnati on January 31, 1900. Marie was also a musician, and the two were leaders in organizing the Cincinnati Chamber Music Society, which held regular concerts in their home at 2147 Madison Road, Cincinnati, which was aptly named "Fiddler's Green." Rudolph H. often played in a string quartet that met in his home.

Rudolph Henry Wurlitzer, age thirty-two, and Marie Richard Wurlitzer. *Courtesy of William E. Griess Jr.*

Rudolph H. and Marie were active in Cincinnati society, and most of their friends were interested in music. For many years, they spent their summers at the Harbor Beach Club near Saginaw, Michigan, where they were the neighbors and friends of the Henry Fords. They also counted among their friends newspaper editor Arthur Brisbane and most of the musicians of the day, including Richard Crooks, Lily Pons, Fritz Kreisler, Rachmaninoff, Percy Grainger, Victor Herbert, Andre Kostelanetz, Piatigorsky, Eugene Goossens, Gabrilowitsch, Albert Spaulding, Ysaÿe, John Charles Thomas, Arthur Rubinstein, Nelson Eddy and many more.

He and Howard went often to New York, always staying at the Ritz. Music events and artists absorbed much of Rudolph H.'s time in Manhattan. In his Cincinnati home, he displayed his collection of photographs of musicians, one of the finest such collections in America. Visiting conductors of the Cincinnati Symphony Orchestra were always entertained by Rudolph H. and Marie. When not following musical pursuits, he loved to walk; he would often walk ten miles on a Sunday in the Cincinnati area.

His childhood friend Bryant Venable told an interesting story about Rudolph H.'s love of the outdoors. Even after he was married and there was a child in the family, he and Venable made a natural history expedition into the mountains of West Virginia. They went up the Ohio River by steamboat to Huntington. From there, they took a small lumber railroad into the hills and made their way up a mountain trail to the village of Logan. Rudolph H. had brought along a Victor talking machine and a dozen popular records, mostly to allay suspicion that they might be revenue officers. During their stay at a hotel in Logan, the Victor machine was a sensation. Before they left, Rudolph H. sold the machine to the wife of the hotel owner.

As a result of the extensive violin study that Rudolph H. made in Europe and in the United States, he developed a reputation as one of the most important authorities on this instrument, both in the United States and abroad. For example, Arthur M. Abell, writing for the *Musical Courier* on June 8, 1918, described a visit that he made in company with esteemed Hungarian violinist Leopold Auer (1845–1930) to the Wurlitzer studio in New York to examine its collection of violins.

*It is a remarkable collection of instruments, by far the greatest I have ever seen at any dealer's in this country. The feature which impressed me most at first was its completeness, for practically every Italian maker of importance is represented; but another scarcely less remarkable feature is the admirable state of preservation, the splendid condition the violins are in. The entire collection of the New York studio numbers something like 200 instruments, but we gave our attention only to the cream of the collection.*

*To me, it was a matter of great surprise to find so many rare specimens of the lutist's art here, for I was not aware that any music house in this country had devoted the time, labor, capital and knowledge necessary in order to get together such a large number of old Italian masterpieces.*

*The knowledge! That is the real secret of the success of the Wurlitzer Collection. Capital can be found, and interest and zeal will furnish time and labor, but the intimate knowledge necessary to find and select genuine masterpieces of these wonderful old craftsmen of the seventeenth and eighteenth centuries—that is a rare attribute. In Rudolph Wurlitzer, the American music trade possesses a great connoisseur, and that factor, more than any other, has contributed to the success of this collection.*

During the visit, Auer asked Rudolph H. to play some of the violins for him. "I would like to hear the tone of the Brothers Amati as played by someone else," said Auer. Abell wrote that Rudolph H. picked up the violin and began to play, not attempting technical feats, but confined himself to a sort of "improvised adagio, testing all the strings in the higher as well as the lower position. I was at once impressed by the fact that he drew a warm, sympathetic tone and that his intonation was perfect."

"Bravo!" Abell quoted Auer as saying when Rudolph H. had finished. "You draw a beautiful tone, and above all, you show that you had at some time in your life been well schooled for you really know how to handle a violin from the viewpoint of artistic tone production, and that is a very rare thing among violin dealers."

According to Abell, the Wurlitzer Collection on the day of his visit with Auer contained several rare violins of the Cremona school, including three Stradivari, two by Antonius and one by Omobono. The Guarnerius family was represented by five specimens, namely Petrus, Joseph Filius Andreas (two) and Petrus Filius Joseph (also two). There were two by Giovanni Batista Ruggeri, a Nicolas Bergonzi, a Brothers Amati, a Laurentius Storiomi and several by lesser-known makers.

Of the Venetian school, there were then in the Wurlitzer Collection two Montagnanas, a Sanctus Seraphin and a fine Matteo Goffriller. Milan was represented by three Gracinon, four Testores, one Carlo Antonio, three Carlo Guiseppes and three Landolfis. Naples was represented by violins from each of three members of the Gagliano family and Mantua by two Camillus Camilli. There were four Tononis from Bologna, two David Techlers from

*Above*: Rudolph H. Wurlitzer (right), Hungarian violinist Leopold Auer and writer Arthur M. Abell (standing) review the rare violin collection in 1918. *Wurlitzer Company Records, Archives Center, National Museum of American History, Smithsonian Institution.*

*Left*: Rudolph Henry Wurlitzer. *Photograph by Blank & Stoller. Courtesy of William E. Griess Jr.*

Rome and four J.B. Guadagninis, as well as a Stainer, two Jacobs, several Klotzes, a Gabrielli quartet and several Lupots. Mr. Abell also noted that Isidore Stern was in immediate charge of the Wurlitzer Collection of violins, Rudolph H. spending most of his time in Cincinnati.

The June 29, 1918 *Musical Courier* referred again to Rudolph H.'s reputation as a connoisseur of violins, noting that "he is recognized as the highest authority in old violins, a study which has been a pleasure to him for years." The same article notes that Cincinnati can boast of Wurlitzer "as the largest music house in the world."

His reputation as an appraiser of violins grew to such an extent that the sheer number of violins taken to him over the years for examination required that he charge a fee for this service.

Although his father and brother Howard considered it more of a hobby than a business, Rudolph H. gradually built up a considerable business in both old and new violins. At one time, the Rudolph Wurlitzer Company had the largest number of Stradivari violins in stock of any firm in America. With the death of department store magnate Rodman Wanamaker (1863–

Rudolph H. and Marie's fortieth wedding anniversary, 1940. The guests are gathered around Rudolph H. and Marie's unusual revolving dining room table at their home, "Fiddler's Green." *Left to right*: Annette Knoop, Elise Richard, Jimmy Hutton, Patsy Griess, Sells Stites, Marie Wurlitzer, Rudolph H. Wurlitzer, Marianne Hutton and Janesy R. Griewe. Photograph by Fred Knoop. *Courtesy of William E. Griess Jr.*

1928), Wurlitzer acquired Wanamaker's prestigious "Cappella" collection of stringed instruments on May 2, 1929.

During World War II, Rudolph H. served as executive secretary of the Hamilton County, Ohio Conservation Board and coordinator of the Hamilton County War Production Board.

Rudolph H. and Marie raised a family of five children. The eldest, Marianne Leonie, born on December 10, 1900, in Cincinnati, married James Morgan Hutton in Cincinnati on November 13, 1926; she died in

Rudolph H. and Marie's children. Marianne (top) with (from left to right) Rembert, Natalie, Janet and Annette. *Courtesy of William E. Griess Jr.*

1969. Janet, born on July 29, 1902, became on January 30, 1925, the wife of Luke Sells Stites, who died on January 20, 1951; Janet died in 1992. Rembert Rudolph was born on March 27, 1904, and died in 1963; he was married to Anna Lee Little. Natalie, known among her friends and relatives as "Patsy," was born on September 29, 1906, and married William Griess in Cincinnati on October 26, 1929; she died in 2000. The youngest, Annette, was born on July 29, 1912, and was the wife of Frederick Knoop. She died in 1970.

Rembert Wurlitzer, Rudolph H.'s son, resigned from the board of directors in 1937 but continued to handle the rare violin business. *Courtesy of William E. Griess Jr.*

It is interesting to note that Rembert, the only son of Rudolph H. and Marie Wurlitzer, shared his parents' love of music. Like his father, he studied in Europe, but before crossing the Atlantic, he worked at the violin shop of J.R. Carlisle in Cincinnati as an apprentice in 1924 for six months. In Europe, he spent eighteen months with the well-known violin craftsman Amédée Dieudonné (1890–1960) at Mirecourt, France, followed by a year in Italy, Germany and England, studying the works of the old violin masters, as well as modern violin making in those countries. In England, he studied under Alfred Hill (1862–1940), the leading violin expert of the world, who asked Rembert to join the firm W.E. Hill and Sons. But Rembert turned down the offer, returning to the family business in America.

Rudolph H. Wurlitzer died on May 27, 1948, and Rembert took over the rare violin business after his father's death.

## *Leonie Jeannette Wurlitzer Eilers*

Leonie Wurlitzer was the second daughter and fourth child of Rudolph and Leonie Wurlitzer. She was born on December 14, 1875, and was two years younger than Rudolph H. The two were very close as brother and sister throughout their lives.

Short, blond, petite and vivacious Leonie and Rudolph H. performed together often, she on the piano and he on the violin. On October 19, 1896, Leonie married Karl Emrich Eilers in Cincinnati. Most of their lives were spent in Pueblo and Denver, Colorado; Salt Lake City; and New York.

Leonie's father-in-law, Frederic Anton Eilers, came to the United States from Germany and was trained as a mining engineer. He was remarkably successful, becoming part owner of smelting companies in Utah, Colorado and Montana. He was one of the early members of the American Institute of Mining Engineers and became its manager and vice-president.

His son Karl was born in Marietta, Ohio, on November 20, 1865, and followed in his father's footsteps. In 1893, Karl Eilers became superintendent of the Colorado Smelting Company at Pueblo, manager in 1899 and director and member of the executive committee of the American Smelting and Refining Company in 1906. He quickly became vice-president in charge of operations and later executive vice-president. The Eilers moved to New York in 1904 and lived for a time at 320 Central Park West at Ninety-first Street. In 1911, they bought a house in Sea Cliff, New York, after having rented places there during summers beginning in 1908.

Karl and Leonie Eilers were both greatly interested in humanitarian projects and did a great amount of entertaining in connection with charity and hospital work. They were the moving force behind the Snow Ball, an annual benefit event held at the Waldorf-Astoria on behalf of the Lenox Hill Hospital.

The Eilers had three children. The eldest was Marguerite Elizabeth, born on July 31, 1898, at Pueblo, Colorado. She was married on October 31, 1931, at Sea Cliff to Andrew Edward Beer, a New York attorney; she died on April 23, 1975. Karl Fritz Eilers was born on September 21, 1899, also at Pueblo; he died on August 1, 1971. He was married on October 1, 1930, in Washington, D.C., to Ann Branson and was employed by the Kennecott Copper Company. Francis Farny Eilers was born on April 4, 1902, in Denver, Colorado. He was married on September 25, 1926, at Waterbury, Connecticut, to Lucille Hopkins, and they lived at Great Neck, Long Island. Francis died on January 26, 1987.

Their mother, Leonie Wurlitzer Eilers, died on January 27, 1947.

## Percival Wurlitzer

A fifth child was born to Rudolph and Leonie Wurlitzer whom they named Percival on November 26, 1877. The child died eight months later, on July 25, 1878, of "cholera infantuum" according to cemetery records.

## Farny Reginald Wurlitzer

By the time Farny Reginald Wurlitzer was born on December 7, 1883, his elder brothers Howard and Rudolph H. were already working in the business; when Farny was school age, they were taking on some of the responsibility and details from the shoulders of their father.

When Farny was about five years old, his older sister Sylvia, then nineteen, was attending a fashionable girls' finishing school in Cincinnati run by Miss Freddin, who also conducted a kindergarten that Farny attended. After kindergarten, he went to the public elementary school, but instead of attending Woodward High School like his brothers, his father sent him for four years to the Cincinnati Technical School, a private school that would be viewed today as a trade or vocational school.

Although Farny's father was no longer a young man, the two seem to have been unusually close. They usually spent time together on Sundays. Rudolph Wurlitzer owned an interest in the Sycamore Street Car Line, a cable line. The two often rode the line on Sundays with Rudolph combining the business of inspection with the pleasure of taking his eight-year-old boy for a jaunt. After the ride, they often went for a walk in Avondale. In later years, the elder Wurlitzer would take Farny to the office on Sundays.

Rudolph would often greet the boy Farny with the words, "Well, Farny, what do you think of Buxtehude?" This reference was actually to Dieterich Buxtehude, a Danish-German organist and composer of the Baroque period. It was a question unintelligible to the boy but one that did not require an answer; it was an affectionate gag line.

Rudolph took each of the sons to the office as soon as they were old enough and gave each the opportunity to do odd jobs. None of the Wurlitzer sons attended college. Their father always succeeded in maintaining a close relationship with them and groomed them for the different roles he expected them to play in the business.

At the time, Rudolph believed that there was a future in the development of automatic music boxes that could be operated with the insertion of a coin. This might have influenced Rudolph's decision to send his youngest son, Farny, to the Cincinnati Technical School. After finishing four years there, Farny continued his studies in Europe. Because of the large variety of trade connections in Europe, Farny needed to become fluent in German and familiar with German business practices. Rudolph decided to take Farny with him to Europe on his next trip and enroll him in a good school. But being an independent, self-sufficient person, Farny wanted to make the trip alone, and he did so before he was eighteen years old, sailing in the summer of 1901.

Farny carried a letter of introduction to the head of the leading commercial school in Hamburg. Farny wanted to be certain that the school would meet his needs, so he questioned the dignified German headmaster at some length, much to the latter's annoyance. The headmaster told him that he had just one vacancy for a student who wanted to "live in," and this was in a room with another boy. Farny objected to this, even though the headmaster assured him that his roommate was a fine boy from a fine South American family. So the interview ended without any agreement being made.

In trying to decide what to do, Farny contacted a family friend, Emil Kuegemann, who was then manager of the Hamburg office of American Radiator Company. Kuegemann assured him that the school was as good as he had been told, and he helped him find lodgings in a *pension* operated by twin sisters. The next day, Farny returned to the school to enter as a student living "outside." But the headmaster, still angry from the questioning of the previous day and Farny's refusal to the living arrangements that he offered, refused to accept him. Farny eventually entered another commercial school, took German lessons and did his best to make the most of his time in Germany. He remained in Hamburg for a year, completing his studies in August 1902.

For many years, Hupfeld Gesellshaft had been the leading German producer of player pianos and orchestrions. Wurlitzer made an offer to buy merchandise from the company and serve as its agent in the United States if Farny were permitted to spend six months in the Hupfeld factory. Hupfeld feared the loss of trade secrets and business and refused to let Farny enter the plant.

So, Howard and Farny made a new arrangement with J.D. Philipps und Söhne, a small manufacturer of orchestrions in Brockenheim, near Frankfurt-am-Main. Wurlitzer ordered four instruments, but the Philipps

Company was so small that they could not make delivery before the following spring. Furthermore, while Philipps had no objection to Farny seeing their manufacturing operations, they insisted that he inspect and pay for each instrument as soon as it was finished.

Since Farny had plenty of time on his hands before the delivery of the last Philipps orchestrion the following spring, he traveled to Switzerland to contact another supplier of the Wurlitzer organization, the Paillard Company at St. Croix, a famous maker of music boxes. The Paillards took Farny in and treated him like a member of the family. The spoke in French, giving Farny the opportunity to better learn the language.

After traveling to St. Petersburg to visit his sister Sylvia, Farny returned to the Philipps firm, inspected the first orchestrion in their order, paid for it and had it shipped to America. Philipps made excellent orchestrions; however, the cash arrangement did not suit the Wurlitzers, and Philipps refused to extend credit to them. Farny decided that something had to be done to impress on the Philipps management that Wurlitzer was a good risk. So, when his father, Rudolph, visited the Philipps plant at Frankfurt-am-Main, Farny saw to it that his father did so in style.

He stayed at the best hotel. He spent several days there and at the Philipps plant, always driving in a fine carriage with a liveried coachman and footman. On his final night in Frankfurt, Rudolph Wurlitzer gave a dinner at the best restaurant for the top people in the Philipps organization. He left it to Farny to arrange the details, and his son spared nothing to make it a grand success, complete with seventy-five-cent cigars wrapped in foil. The Philipps management was properly impressed, and from then on, there was never any question of credit. Philipps made Pianella orchestrions, which were imported into the United States as the Wurlitzer PianOrchestra.

After settling the business at the Philipps plant, Farny journeyed with his father and mother to visit the old hometowns of his father at Schöneck and Markneukirchen. He met his great-uncle Wilhelm Hochmuth, the man who had loaned his father passage money to America, and two of his father's sisters, Aunt Henriette Adelheid and Aunt Friedericke.

Next, Farny went to Lyon, France, and spent about six months in a brass musical instrument plant that was one of the chief Wurlitzer suppliers, Pelisson Guinot Blanchon et Cie., at 273 Cours Lafayette. While in Lyon, Farny lived with a French family, spending mornings in the plant and the afternoons taking lessons from a French teacher. Eugene DeKleist, a man who would figure large in Farny's future, invited him to travel to Switzerland with him for a vacation. By this time, DeKleist had been selling musical instruments to the Wurlitzer organization from his factory in North Tonawanda, New York. After his sojourn in Lyon, Farny traveled on to Paris and London, returning to Cincinnati in April 1904, ready to go to work.

On his return to the home office, Farny became smitten with Miss Grace Keene, his brother Howard's secretary. She had been employed by Howard for some time in a confidential capacity, handling his correspondence for weeks at a time when Howard was in Europe or elsewhere. When Howard learned of his young brother's romantic interest in his secretary, he reacted by firing her. Farny and Grace courted for about five years, marrying in a quiet ceremony in Christ Church Cathedral (Episcopal) in Cincinnati on August 27, 1910. The couple honeymooned in Europe and in St. Petersburg.

While each of the three brothers occupied leadership positions in the company, Farny's strength was his technical knowledge and his ability to use it for financial gain. He moved from Cincinnati around 1909 to supervise the newly acquired DeKleist Musical Instrument Manufacturing Company and to expand it into a new Wurlitzer plant in North Tonawanda, New York. Farny was directly responsible for the manufacture of various automatic

musical instruments (coin pianos and orchestrions) and the famous "Mighty Wurlitzer" theater organ. He became president of the company on July 30, 1932, and, in 1942, chairman of the board. He remained as chairman emeritus from 1966 until his death on May 6, 1972, in Kenmore, New York. His wife, Grace, had already died in 1968. They had no children. The founding of the Rudolph Wurlitzer Company in 1856 by Rudolph and the death of his son Farny Wurlitzer spanned a period of an astonishing 116 years. The Farny R. Wurlitzer Foundation was established in 1949 in Sycamore, Illinois, to promote musical education, and the foundation today boasts over $4 million in assets.

Farny Reginald Wurlitzer. *Courtesy of David Eilers and North Tonawanda History Museum.*

All four of the male Wurlitzer children (including the infant Percival) and their spouses are buried in Cincinnati's Spring Grove Cemetery. There is a large Wurlitzer plot with a bench inscribed with the family name, but Howard and his wife, Helene, have a separate plot some distance away in a different section of the cemetery.

According to Don Rand, Tracy Newman, Art Reblitz and Terry Hathaway, writing for the online site mechanicalmusicpress.com, the unexpected death of Howard Wurlitzer is borne out by the fact that the cemetery plot for Howard and his family was owned by his wife, Helene, presumably because she had to acquire it in haste. But it's unclear as to why she found it necessary or even desirable to own a separate plot for herself and Howard and their unmarried daughter, Luise, when there was already a spacious Wurlitzer family area in the same cemetery. This separate plot is secluded and essentially hidden under a wooden trellis overgrown with a vine. Howard Wurlitzer was an energetic and aggressive businessman, and there were rumors that he was disliked by some people within the company. This causes speculation that there was also a rift in the family, but what the rift might have been, or if there were some kind of permanent estrangement, remains unknown.

# 7

# THE SONS ENTER THE BUSINESS

From 1856 to 1890, Rudolph Wurlitzer succeeded in pyramiding his initial investment of $700 of savings into a very profitable business with sales every year amounting to six figures. But this was still a one-man enterprise. Rudolph guided the business and made the buying trips to Europe. He evolved the business from a one-room "warehouse" to eventually occupy the entire building at 123 Main Street. From 1878 to 1890, the firm occupied 115 Main Street and then moved to 121 East Fourth Street.

By 1890, Rudolph Wurlitzer was fifty-nine years old. Up to this time, his two closest business associates were his brother Anton Wurlitzer and Adolph Charles Strobel, the husband of Marguerite Farny, his wife's sister. Although Rudolph owned the business, it was known in the trade for many years as Rudolph Wurlitzer & Brother, and its trademark even as late as 1912 was "RWB."

But Rudolph dreamed that his three sons would be trained in the business and eventually take it over. Expecting a more complex business relationship, he incorporated the company in 1890 for $200,000. The original stock record book shows that Certificate No. 1 was issued on March 29, 1890, to Rudolph Wurlitzer for one thousand shares. On the same day, two hundred shares were issued to Anton Wurlitzer, and one hundred shares were issued to A.C. Strobel. Five shares were also issued to each of his five children. The

Main offices and showrooms of the House of Wurlitzer, 121 East Fourth
Street, Cincinnati. This was the company's headquarters beginning in 1891.
The building was destroyed by fire in 1904, but the company rebuilt at the
same location and dedicated the new building in 1906. *From* The Music
Trades; *courtesy of William Griess Jr.*

Wurlitzer brothers with their father about 1906: Howard (left), Farny (standing), Rudolph Henry (right), Howard's son Raimund (center, second from right) and Rudolph H.'s son Rembert (with toy rabbit). *Courtesy of William E. Griess Jr.*

next year, Howard was issued an additional ten shares, presumably because he had actually entered the business.

The documents of incorporation stated that the business was established for the purpose of "importing, manufacturing, selling and dealing in musical instruments and fancy goods of various kinds." Incorporators included Rudolph, Anton, their brother-in-law Strobel, Howard and George A. Metzel, the cashier and office manager who was with the company for thirty years but was never a stockholder.

Anton retired from the company on June 1, 1897, and Rudolph purchased his stock interest of two hundred shares for $30,000; he also bought the one hundred shares owned by A.C. Strobel. With Anton Wurlitzer and Adolph Strobel out of the company, Rudolph's son Howard became vice-president in 1899, and his son Rudolph H. became secretary and treasurer. This was still a simple family business and would remain so for about three more decades.

However, during Rudolph's time in charge, he also invested in traction lines in and near Cincinnati, western mines, a mine in Panama and other ventures. Unfortunately, these outside ventures were mostly failures. His musical instrument business continued to be a success, allowing him to indulge in the luxury of travel and making rather risky investments.

As soon as the three boys were old enough, they worked the store and office in their spare time. Their father thought that there was no education that could take the place of experience. In his view, it would be more advantageous for his sons to be familiar with the sources of supply of musical instruments and how to deal with them on their own turf than to earn college degrees.

However, Rudolph did support the musical training received by Sylvia and Rudolph H. in Berlin and in the United States. It was appropriate for a girl in those days to be trained in music, possibly providing her with a living as a music teacher should the need ever arise. And for Rudolph H., his reputation as an accomplished violinist gave prestige to the business.

If the sons had been college educated, it is interesting to speculate how they might have foreseen the dangers of internal strife in the 1920s and been better equipped to handle it. They might have been able to handle the business in the days of the Depression without having to go outside the family for leadership. On the other hand, as college men, they might not have had that hardheaded business sense and aggressiveness to carry the business to great success during their three decades of management.

When Howard received his first shares of stock from his father in 1890, he was still under nineteen years old, but he had already been working full time for the business for about two years. Rudolph H. was not quite seventeen, and Farny was only seven. It was not long before Howard's grasp of the complex details, rivaled only by his father's attention to detail, set him on course for eventually replacing his father.

At times when Rudolph was traveling in Europe, usually every other year, Howard and Rudolph H. kept in touch with him by letters and cables, writing in great detail on purchases and conditions of the business.

An example of this is how the family handled a problem with shipments of bugles and trumpets that Wurlitzer sold to the government, having been misled by the European supplier. In a letter on June 11, 1898, to his father, Howard wrote that the quartermaster's department had rejected a shipment of artillery bugles "because they were not correct."

The government letter stated:

*I regret to be obliged to advise you that the B-flat bugles, shipped by you, invoiced as 60, are held subject to your order. 35 are rejected on account of the E being flat and 22 for not being in pitch with the standard sample, the E being flat. The remaining 3, while fairly in tune, are not in pitch with the U.S. standard, being slightly flat. It is very important that these Bugles should all be identical, as they are often played in concert, and a slight difference in pitch, or the irregularity of one note, renders them useless.*

Howard asked his father to straighten the matter out with Reidel, the German supplier, saying that Reidel still had the "standard sample. Please see to it that we get them at once," he wrote, "and impress it on them that they must be right, otherwise we cannot use them."

Three days later, S.W. Monfort, a bugle specialist with Wurlitzer in Cincinnati, explained the trouble in detail.

*We find after close inspection, that there was so much lead left on the inside of them that if you would slide a slug in at the small opening, or where the mouthpiece fits, when it came around to the joints, or in fact any portion of the horn although the caliber was much larger, the lead was so thick that the slug could not pass through; hence the flatness of the instrument. From the bugles that [we] looked at, [we] took nearly a thimble full of lead out of each one, so you can see the instruments are not of clear bore, hence it has not only deadened the tone, but made the lower notes flat. Again, the mouthpiece bore is too small to bring out the low notes as clear as they should be. Mr. Joseph is reaming out each one of the mouthpieces as well as making the bore a trifle larger.*

*We believe we have discovered the difference between the French and the German manufacturers, and the difference lies in this one point in particular. The French see that their instruments are clear bore, or in other words, are cleaned out nicely, while the German manufacturer pays no attention to the inside of the instrument. If you can catch the manufacturer in time, it would be well to call his attention to these points before he ships the instruments. If this is not done, there will be an expense of 15 to 20 cents to put them in condition so they may be accepted by the Government.*

By 1898, the creation of the company catalogues had become one of Howard's major responsibilities. In 1879, the catalogue contained 216 pages, but in 1898, it was a book of 344 pages, contained hundreds of illustrations

# SAXOPHONE TRIMMINGS.

### PADS FOR SAXOPHONES.

| No. | | Per Dozen. |
|---|---|---|
| 2775 | Kid Leather, Assorted Sizes | $ 1 25 |

### BARBU REEDS FOR SAXOPHONES.

| No. | | Per Dozen. |
|---|---|---|
| 2777 | Best Barbu for B♭ Soprano and E♭ Alto | $ 2 50 |
| 2778 | " " " B♭ Tenor and B♭ Baritone | 4 00 |

### MOUTHPIECES FOR SAXOPHONES.

| No. | | Each. |
|---|---|---|
| 2780 | B♭ Soprano, Grenadilla Wood, with Reed Holder | $ 4 50 |
| 2781 | E♭ Alto " " " " | 7 50 |
| 2782 | B♭ Tenor " " " " | 8 00 |
| 2783 | B♭ Baritone " " " " | 8 50 |

### REED HOLDERS FOR SAXOPHONE.

| No. | | | Each. |
|---|---|---|---|
| 2786 | For Soprano | Brass, | $ 62 |
| 2787 | " Alto | " | 75 |
| 2788 | " Tenor | " | 95 |
| 2789 | " Baritone | " | 1 15 |

# SPEAKING TRUMPETS.

No. 2811.

| No. | | | Each. |
|---|---|---|---|
| 2810 | Fireman's Horn, with Reed | Brass Polished, | $ 7 00 |
| | The Same | Triple Silver Plated, Burnished, | 12 50 |
| 2811 | " or Fog Horn, with Adjustable Reed | Brass, | 13 50 |
| | " | Triple Silver Plated, Burnished, | 19 00 |

# U. S. ARMY REGULATION TRUMPETS.

No. 2815.

## F TRUMPET.

| No. | | | Each. |
|---|---|---|---|
| 2815 | F Trumpet, or Infantry | Brass, | $ 5 00 |
| | The Same | Nickel Plated, | 6 50 |
| | " | Triple Silver Plated, Burnished, | 10 75 |
| 2816 | F Trumpet, with C Crook, for Cavalry | Brass, | 7 25 |
| | The Same | Nickel Plated, | 9 00 |
| | " | Triple Silver Plated, Burnished, | 14 00 |

*This page and next*: Pages 80 and 81 of Wurlitzer's 1890 catalogue showing their offerings of military trumpets.

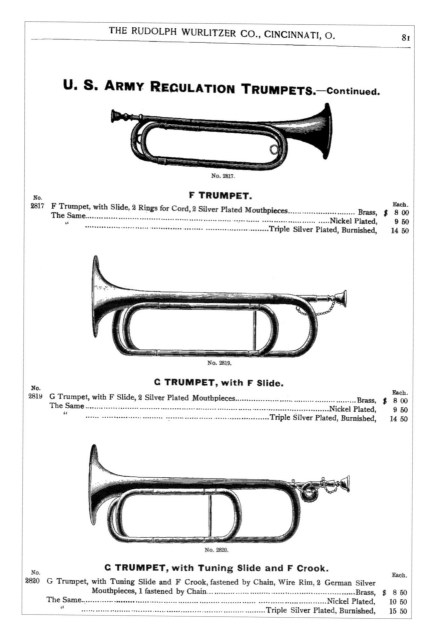

## U. S. ARMY REGULATION TRUMPETS.—Continued.

No. 2817.

### F TRUMPET.

| No. | | Each. |
|---|---|---|
| 2817 | F Trumpet, with Slide, 2 Rings for Cord, 2 Silver Plated Mouthpieces.......................... Brass, | $ 8 00 |
| | The Same......................................................................................................Nickel Plated, | 9 50 |
| " | ..........................................................................Triple Silver Plated, Burnished, | 14 50 |

No. 2819.

### G TRUMPET, with F Slide.

| No. | | Each. |
|---|---|---|
| 2819 | G Trumpet, with F Slide, 2 Silver Plated Mouthpieces.................................................Brass, | $ 8 00 |
| | The Same...........................................................................................................Nickel Plated, | 9 50 |
| " | ....................................................................................Triple Silver Plated, Burnished, | 14 50 |

No. 2820.

### G TRUMPET, with Tuning Slide and F Crook.

| No. | | Each. |
|---|---|---|
| 2820 | G Trumpet, with Tuning Slide and F Crook, fastened by Chain, Wire Rim, 2 German Silver Mouthpieces, 1 fastened by Chain..............................................................................Brass, | $ 8 50 |
| | The Same..................................................................................................Nickel Plated, | 10 50 |
| " | ..................................................................................Triple Silver Plated, Burnished, | 15 50 |

and was an inch and a half thick. Perhaps better than anything else, these catalogues show the complexity of the Wurlitzer business at the time.

In addition to band instruments, pianos and orchestrions, the 1898 catalogue had a page of "Swiss Musical Boxes" of the pin-cylinder type with prices from $18 to $200, several with a "zither attachment" that would play from six to twelve "airs." An odd group of mechanical musical instruments, which would be collectors' items today, included musical decanters, pitchers, beer mugs, family albums and a musical majolica beer jug. There were also "pipe hand organs for street, saloon and circus" at $300 each. They were portable and carried two pinned cylinders, capable of playing "8 airs" each, with "29 Keys, Flute and Trumpets."

Son Rudolph H.'s letters to his father focused on violins. In a letter of May 3, 1898, he wrote, "I would advise your buying some old violins—but only unrepaired instruments to cost at the utmost 100 Marks. We can repair them to better advantage here, because they do not take pains in repairing them in Europe and generally spoil them by revarnishing and poor repairing." Two days later, Rudolph H. wrote to his father, "When you go to London, you might stop to see Hill and Son and Hart and Son in reference to possibly sending us in the future a few fine violins on sale. I think perhaps we could also handle some of the books published by Hill. I find that there is a fair demand for books of this kind."

Although all three sons became familiar with all phases of the business, each developed his own special interests. Howard's strength was the financial side, and he constantly sought ways to expand the business. He saw the great possibilities in the automatic (coin-operated) musical instrument business, but Farny was the one to handle the details of development and manufacture of these instruments, particularly the phonograph. Rudolph H.'s interest in the violin made it possible for the Rudolph Wurlitzer Company to build up the greatest collection of old violins in the United States and the finest collection of Stradivari in the world and to eventually acquire the famous Wanamaker Collection. Rudolph H. later specialized in the talking machine business, initiating a lucrative arrangement with Victor Talking Machine Company. For many years, Wurlitzer carried the Victor line exclusively.

Around 1900, Rudolph the founder began to release control of the business and indulged his desire to travel, both for business and pleasure. He made trips west and to Panama in connection with his mining investments.

By the time Farny took his place in the family business, his brothers, Howard and Rudolph H., were firmly in charge of its management. Farny would often have lunch with his father on a typical workday; Howard more likely would have lunch with his uncle Henry Farny in his studio across the street and Rudolph H. with some of his musical cronies.

On Sundays, Farny and his father usually went to the office for an hour or two to open the mail. It was on such a Sunday, November 20, 1904, that a fire broke out next door to the Wurlitzer building, a big fire that burned for twelve hours before it was put out and resulted in a loss of $483,000. There was a five-column, front-page drawing of the fire with details of the disaster running into several columns in the *Commercial Tribune* of Cincinnati the next day. The newspaper credited young Farny Wurlitzer with discovering the blaze.

It was a disastrous fire for the city and for Wurlitzer. Thirty-four businesses in all were involved in losses, and twelve buildings bordering on Bank Alley were ruined. Although it was a difficult experience for the aging Rudolph Wurlitzer, to his sons it was a challenge. The Rudolph Wurlitzer Company announced its move to temporary quarters at 412-414-416 Elm Street. About three weeks later, on December 16, 1904, the company advertised its new quarters at 10 and 12 West Fourth Street, a building with six floors. "We were fired out," the main caption of the advertisement read, and they featured a completely new stock, including Cable-Nelson pianos, Victor talking machines and Edison phonographs. It was a good test for the sons, and they met it effectively. The company built a new headquarters on the site of the old, moving into it in 1907.

Farny became familiar enough with the business by late 1904 that he took to the road on selling trips, calling on Wurlitzer dealers in the south, west and northwest. The company was expanding under the management of the young men. Rudolph, the founder, attended his last board of directors meeting on April 25, 1913.

Through all these years, the Rudolph Wurlitzer Company was still very much a family-run business. Only insignificant amounts of stock were held by other company executives, employees or those outside the organization before 1930; members of the family held large amounts of preferred stock.

In addition to the expansion of retail outlets and lucrative arrangements for handling the goods of domestic and foreign manufacturers such as the Victor Talking Machine and American Piano Company, a large part of Wurlitzer's success lay in the development of special projects, such as one with Eugene DeKleist.

DeKleist was born "von Kleist" in Dusseldorf about 1867, replacing "von" with "de" while living in Belgium. He was an accomplished pianist and organist and worked for Limonaire Frères in Paris and London for a time. The company made merry-go-round organs and music cylinders.

In 1892, while working in London, DeKleist met William Herschell, whose brothers George and Allan manufactured carousels in North Tonawanda, New York. Since Limonaire Frères was an agent for German woodcarvers who produced carousel horses, Herschell placed a large order to be shipped to the Armitage Company in North Tonawanda.

Eugene DeKleist (back row, fourth from right) poses sometime after 1892 with officials of the Armitage-Herschell Company, an early client of his North Tonawanda Barrel Organ Factory. Also in the back row are George Herschell (third from right) and James Armitage (to the left of the young boy). *Courtesy of Ron Bopp.*

Within a short time, Herschell asked DeKleist to travel to America to visit the factory in North Tonawanda. High tariffs had made the purchase of carousel barrel organs abroad almost prohibitive, and the Armitage-Herschell Company was anxious to obtain a source in the United States. This trip resulted in DeKleist's decision to immigrate to America permanently and start the North Tonawanda Barrel Organ Factory in 1893.

DeKleist bought the machinery of the defunct Hewitt Furniture Company of North Tonawanda and was in business, starting with seven men, and soon had the rather limited "barrel-organ" business neatly buttoned up. Seeking to expand, he contacted Howard Wurlitzer in 1897 to sell him on the idea that Wurlitzer should sell his product. Howard declined his proposal to sell barrel organs, but if DeKleist could develop a coin-operated piano, Wurlitzer would likely be able to find a large market for it.

During the next decade, DeKleist produced and sold to Wurlitzer several different types of automatic, coin-operated pianos and other musical instruments. He obtained more than sixty patents during his lifetime. Wurlitzer first sold the enormously successful Tonophone, an automatic piano first operated with a wooden cylinder, similar to the barrel organs already made by DeKleist. Each cylinder had ten tunes.

One of DeKleist's catalogues for 1901 shows that he had changed the name of the business from the North Tonawanda Barrel Organ Factory to the DeKleist Musical Instrument Manufacturing Company. It listed pianos with forty-eight hammers, playing ten tunes, "with nickel-in-the-slot attachment extra." It showed orchestrions and other instruments, operated by perforated paper at prices from $200 to $8,000. There were reed organs, flute organs, organs with wooden trumpets (up to $725), clarionette organs, "harmonipans" and a wide variety of military band organs ranging up to $2,700 in cost.

Following the Tonophone in 1903 was the Pianino, a forty-four-note piano with paper-roll operation. The roll was motor driven and at first gave a selection of five and, later, ten tunes.

In order to expand his facilities, DeKleist had incorporated his business in 1901; about 1907, DeKleist expanded by buying the rights to manufacture a roll changer from Verstrallen and Alter of New York City. This device automatically changed six piano rolls, each roll carrying five tunes. DeKleist produced this device at his factory in North Tonawanda.

Eugene DeKleist prospered with the business the Rudolph Wurlitzer Company gave him. In 1905, he became president of the North Tonawanda Council and in 1907 mayor of North Tonawanda. These were each two-year terms that required him to move his business office from the musical instrument works to the Sheldon Hotel downtown. Apparently the social and public demands of these political offices kept him from paying attention to his band organ business, and the quality of the DeKleist products and service started to decline. As he gradually began to lose interest in his company, he left its operation to his son August. Eugene also had a heart ailment contributing to the problem. Howard Wurlitzer gave DeKleist an ultimatum: either sell out to the Rudolph Wurlitzer Company or prepare for competition from them. So, in July 1908, Wurlitzer bought the DeKleist business, organizing it as a new company, the Rudolph Wurlitzer Manufacturing Company. DeKleist died July 28, 1913, while crossing the Pyrenees traveling from Málaga, Spain, to Berlin.

Howard Wurlitzer soon realized that he could not efficiently manage the North Tonawanda facility from his office in Cincinnati. So, in early 1909, Howard sent his youngest brother, Farny, to North Tonawanda to gradually

*Above*: Howard Wurlitzer (left) and Eugene DeKleist. *Wurlitzer Company Records, Archives Center, National Museum of American History, Smithsonian Institution.*

*Right*: Farny Wurlitzer with silent film actress Priscilla Dean at the North Tonawanda factory in 1925. *From* Encyclopedia of the American Theatre Organ, Volume 3.

take over the plant's management. Farny and his new wife moved there permanently in 1910.

Farny had first met Eugene DeKleist in Lyon, France, in 1903 and had visited the DeKleist household on Goundry Street in North Tonawanda in 1904. Thus, it was natural that Farny was to manage this new Wurlitzer expansion. Farny advanced DeKleist's ideas of the sales possibilities for the coin-operated musical devices.

Meanwhile, Howard and Rudolph H. were also branching out. Just before World War I, they acquired a 40 percent interest in the American Welte Company, which operated a piano and a player piano plant at Poughkeepsie. The pianos used the Welte expression device for its reproducing pianos, and Wurlitzer found this to be a very valuable asset.

In 1909, the Rudolph Wurlitzer Company began to buy stock in the American Piano Company, which owned factories in different cities, including Rochester, Boston and Baltimore, with a main office in New York, and produced pianos under the names of Mason and Hamlin, Knabe, Chickering and Foster and Armstrong. Wurlitzer eventually acquired about 26 percent of the American Piano Company stock. The player piano was all the rage throughout those years, and the American Piano Company was immensely successful.

But in 1925, the Wurlitzer men began to question the future of the player piano. Phonographs were becoming more popular, and radio was about to take off. So, they sold the American Piano Company stock to a Wall Street syndicate, providing Wurlitzer with a $1 million profit. Two years later, the player piano fad had collapsed.

During the years leading up to 1929, Wurlitzer purchased stock in the Apollo Piano Company, band instrument maker C.G. Conn Ltd., Buescher Band Instrument Company and the Martin Band Instrument Company. An even more significant purchase made by Wurlitzer was the Melville Clark Piano Company in DeKalb, Illinois. (Melville Clark Piano Company retained the part of its business that manufactured the Q.R.S. Music Roll and moved it to a factory near Chicago.)

It signaled the end of an era for the Rudolph Wurlitzer Company when Howard Wurlitzer attended his last meeting of the board of directors on March 27, 1928. He retired on May 1 with a pension of $1,000 a month.

The company's early arrangement to sell Regina music boxes in volume from 1893 to 1903 was one of its most successful ventures. The purchase of Eugene DeKleist's business in North Tonawanda profoundly affected the future of the entire business, and the long and mutually profitable arrangement with Victor in the sale of phonographs also added to the company's profits and prestige. Wurlitzer's coming association with Robert Hope-Jones, giving him a free hand to develop a pipe organ for the entertainment field, helped give Wurlitzer worldwide name recognition before the advent of talking pictures. The founder had begun with a $700 investment in 1856. By the end of 1927, his sons had expanded the company's value to $10.5 million.

# 8
# TRANSITIONS

Few if any businesses escaped the consequences of the worldwide economic downturn that began with the stock market crash on Black Tuesday, October 29, 1929. Overnight, the tactics that the Wurlitzer organization had embraced became known as overexpansion.

The Rudolph Wurlitzer Company experienced a deterioration of its securities portfolio. Its stocks held at a cost of $1,577,744.25 were given a book value on March 31, 1934, of only $547,270.00. By November 15, 1934, their value dropped even further, to a market value of $174,331.87.

Of course, thousands of other businesses were in a similar predicament. Blue-chip stocks were then being traded on the New York Stock Exchange at a mere tenth of the price Wurlitzer management had paid for them.

By 1934, sales in Wurlitzer stores had also dropped alarmingly from the lush days of the 1920s. The branch stores, geared to a high volume of business, were swamped by difficulties, including diminishing sales and profits and overwhelming overhead. Wurlitzer had gone into the manufacture of radios, furniture and refrigerators but never was able to compete successfully with the other producers in the field.

But there were other difficult conditions that the Wurlitzer management faced. The huge worldwide market for Wurlitzer pipe organs, used mostly as accompaniment for silent movies, dried up with the advent of talking pictures and by 1934 had nearly ended. For years, Wurlitzer had a large business in manufacturing pianos and player pianos, but with the wide acceptance of radio music in the 1920s, not many people were buying

*Left*: *House of the Farnys* in the Guémar village near Ribeauvillé, Alsace. This was the Farny ancestral home, dating from 1355. This 1896 watercolor by Henry Farny was reproduced in the Wurlitzer centennial cookbook, *A Book of Recipes Covering Three Generations of the Wurlitzer Family and the Wives of Present Business Associates.*

*Below*: *Our Old Home on the Tionesta* watercolor painted in 1913 by Henry F. Farny.

*Theodore Roosevelt Sage Grouse Hunting* by Henry F. Farny. Painting, watercolor and gouache on paperboard, unknown date.

Henry Farny's 1904 painting *The Song of the Talking Wire* depicts an Indian named Long Day listening at a telegraph pole so that he could tell fellow Indians that he had heard spirit voices over the wires, thus proving his ability to become a medicine man, according to art historian Denny Carter. *From Henry Farny by Denny Carter.*

*Right*: Wurlitzer sold band instruments for most of its existence, such as this trumpet outfit shown in a catalogue from about 1915. *Wurlitzer Company Records, Archives Center, National Museum of American History, Smithsonian Institution.*

*Below*: Two pages of Wurlitzer's 1916 catalogue show twenty-four retail stores and its North Tonawanda factory. *Wurlitzer Company Records, Archives Center, National Museum of American History, Smithsonian Institution.*

Wurlitzer's display on Main Street in Disneyland in 1956. Wurlitzer provided all of the keyboard instruments for the park. *Wurlitzer Company Records, Archives Center, National Museum of American History, Smithsonian Institution.*

Three Regina music boxes with disc changers: coin-operated Sublima Corona Style 34 (left); Sublima Corona Style 31 (center); Orchestral Corona Style 8 (right). Style 31 played twenty-and-one-quarter-inch discs; the other two used twenty-seven-inch discs. Manufactured in Rahway, New Jersey, these music boxes, fitted with coin slots, put Wurlitzer on its way to becoming a force in the world of automatic music. *From the Sanfilippo Collection. From* The Golden Age of Automatic Musical Instruments, *copyright 2001, Arthur A. Reblitz, Mechanical Music Press. Used with permission.*

The Pianino was one of Wurlitzer's best sellers throughout the nickelodeon era. *From the Krughoff Collection. From* The Golden Age of Automatic Musical Instruments, *copyright 2001, Arthur A. Reblitz. Used with permission.*

This is an example of a Violin-Flute Pianino from about 1920. The interior view shows the violin pipes and flute pipes in the lower section of the instrument. *From the Krughoff Collection. From* The Golden Age of Automatic Musical Instruments, *copyright 2001, Arthur A. Reblitz. Used with permission.*

A rare Wurlitzer brass Caliola calliope in a style popular from 1929 to 1942. Similar to a band organ, which has many ranks of wood and metal pipes, a calliope has just one rank of large brass whistles. *From the Sanfilippo Collection. From* The Golden Age of Automatic Musical Instruments, *copyright 2001, Arthur A. Reblitz. Used with permission.*

The Wurlitzer Bijou Orchestra from 1913. It contained a forty-four-note piano with violin pipes, xylophone, snare drum and a roll changer. *Sanfilippo Collection. From* The Golden Age of Automatic Musical Instruments, *copyright 2001, Arthur A. Reblitz. Used with permission.*

The Wurlitzer Automatic Harp, Style B from about 1908. *From the Krughoff Collection. From* The Golden Age of Automatic Musical Instruments, *copyright 2001, Arthur A. Reblitz. Used with permission.*

A Wurlitzer Style 16 Mandolin PianOrchestra from 1913. *Sanfilippo Collection. From* The Golden Age of Automatic Musical Instruments, *copyright 2001, Arthur A. Reblitz. Used with permission.*

*Above*: A postcard image depicting the console of the Wurlitzer theater organ in the Riviera Theatre, North Tonawanda, New York. *Courtesy of North Tonawanda History Museum.*

*Left*: This magazine advertisement from 1947 was designed to appeal to parents.

*Right*: The Wurlitzer Model 200 electronic piano allowed a student to practice without bothering others. *Wurlitzer Company Records, Archives Center, National Museum of American History, Smithsonian Institution.*

*Below*: Wurlitzer advertising stated, "Hundreds of public and parochial schools, colleges and universities use the Wurlitzer Music Laboratory for class piano instruction." *Wurlitzer Company Records, Archives Center, National Museum of American History, Smithsonian Institution.*

Model 200 Portable Electronic Piano

Thanks to the popular new Wurlitzer Electronic Piano with earphones, silent piano practice is now possible.

*For your enjoyment of the best in music...* WURLĪTZER

This 1941 advertisement for Catalin Corporation featured a Wurlitzer Model 850 jukebox, known as the "Peacock."

This advertisement by artist Albert Dorne shows the most popular jukebox of all time, the Wurlitzer Model 1015 of 1946, featuring animated side pilasters, three-dimensional plastics and bubble tubes. It was heavily promoted by Wurlitzer; this advertisement also features the Johnny One Note logo. *Courtesy of North Tonawanda History Museum.*

Wurlitzer's Model 1015 jukebox was the all-time sales leader; According to Rick Botts, 56,246 of them were shipped from the factory between 1946 and 1947. It has eight bubble tubes and two revolving color cylinders for animation. *Courtesy of Gert Almind.*

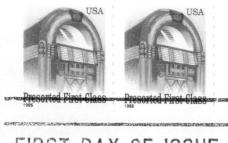

FIRST DAY OF ISSUE

In 1995, the United States Postal Service issued a first-class stamp to commemorate the fiftieth anniversary of the most popular jukebox in history, the Wurlitzer Model 1015. Although the stamp showed no denomination, it had a twenty-five-cent value. *Courtesy of Greg Dumais.*

## Juke Box

Popular, automated record player,
instant music with the drop of a coin.

An advertisement by Albert Dorne depicts the Wurlitzer Model 1100 of 1947, Fuller's final jukebox design for Wurlitzer. *Courtesy of North Tonawanda History Museum.*

Wurlitzer's Model 1250, produced in 1950, played 78-rpm records but could be converted to play 45s or 33⅓s. *Courtesy of North Tonawanda History Museum.*

In 1965, Wurlitzer advertised its new Model 2910 jukebox in a blond cabinet. *Courtesy of North Tonawanda History Museum.*

Separate advertisements were issued aimed toward white or African American audiences. Also shown is a remote selection unit, common to Wurlitzer jukeboxes from the beginning, along with the stereophonic version of Wurlitzer's Johnny One Note logo. *Courtesy of North Tonawanda History Museum.*

Wurlitzer's Cabaret jukebox of 1972, resembling a home stereo system of the time. *Courtesy of North Tonawanda History Museum.*

In the 1970s, Deutsche Wurlitzer produced Carousel model jukeboxes that played cassette tapes instead of discs. *Courtesy of North Tonawanda History Museum.*

In 1986, Deutsche Wurlitzer introduced the OMT (One More Time) jukebox, an updated version of the iconic Model 1015. Jukebox manufacturing was discontinued in 2013. *Courtesy of Deutsche Wurlitzer.*

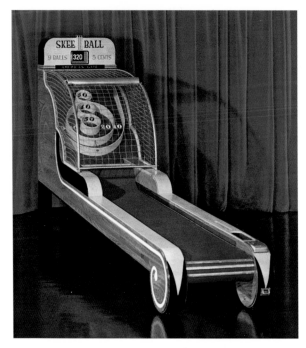

A 1936 Wurlitzer sales brochure for Skee-Ball arcade games shows the game as redesigned by Paul Fuller. *Wurlitzer Company Records, Archives Center, National Museum of American History, Smithsonian Institution.*

pianos of any kind. Sales fell flat as people opted to put food on the table rather than buy musical instruments.

Further complicating the situation was the fact that Prohibition had sharply curtailed sales of coin-operated musical instruments, used primarily in pubs and other drinking establishments. By the 1930s, the sales of these instruments had practically been abandoned.

In the early 1930s, Wurlitzer lacked working capital. The uneasy relationship between the two eldest brothers contributed indirectly to this problem. Both had excellent taste, were fond of music, had energy and imagination and held detailed knowledge of the business but were vitally dissimilar. Howard was more stable and sharper in a business deal. Rudolph H. was more easygoing and likely to take a chance and be carried away by optimism.

Unfortunately, neither of the two eldest brothers could abide his nephews taking on a role in the business, although their sons were eager to take on the role. It fell to youngest brother Farny to soothe hard feelings. Farny was by nature a peacemaker and did his best to keep Wurlitzer management operating on a sound, untroubled basis. It may well have been a help that he had spent practically all his time for years managing the North Tonawanda plant, a distance that gave him added perspective on the central management in Cincinnati. Furthermore, he did not have sons or daughters to complicate the business situation.

Howard withdrew from the company in 1927 when he saw no future in the business with Rudolph H. in the dominant role. Howard's sister Leonie decided to support his view. Sylvia decided to support Rudolph H. The youngest son, Farny, had become vitally important, more so than anyone else at the time because he had the manufacturing experience that the others lacked. He realized that the withdrawal of Howard and Leonie from the family business was inevitable.

The three remaining family members, Sylvia, Rudolph H. and Farny, at the time did not have sufficient personal funds to buy out Howard and Leonie. This was resolved by the purchase and retirement of the stock interests of the two retiring members by the firm for the sum of $4,200,000. This turned out to be financially unsound, since it dangerously reduced the company's working capital for its far-flung and complex operations.

Rudolph H. had made personal real estate investments in and around Cincinnati and other interests that now hampered his relationship with the company of which he was now head. Eventually, he turned over most of his personal real estate assets to the company.

Reuben C. Rolfing in 1938. *Courtesy of North Tonawanda History Museum.*

So, the combination of the onset of the Depression, cultural changes in the modes of music making and delivery, family squabbles and poor investments brought the Rudolph Wurlitzer Company to a crisis in early 1934. Wurlitzer owed approximately $2 million to six different banks, chief of which was the First National Bank of Chicago. Seeking to resolve the crisis, the management of First National took the initiative in late April 1934 to contact Reuben C. Rolfing, then living in San Marino, a suburb of Los Angeles, who was in the construction business. First National president Bentley G. McCloud asked him if he would be interested in heading up the reorganization of a business in the East. Mr. Rolfing agreed to travel to Chicago to discuss it.

At the meeting, Rolfing realized that what he was being asked to do was not pleasant. The problems involved six banks, money, the Wurlitzer family management and thousands of employees and hundreds of dealers under the most adverse national economic conditions. Rolfing had a reputation for salvaging businesses experiencing difficult management and financial problems, having already dealt with the merger of five companies in the agricultural field and solving a bad situation in the radio manufacturing field. Rolfing agreed to step in as general manager, and First National gave him *carte blanche* to reestablish, if possible, the Rudolph Wurlitzer Company.

This was a gamble for the six banks to take and a big gamble for R.C. Rolfing. If he succeeded, he would benefit in terms of money and management prestige. If he failed, the failure would be sad for everyone, especially the members of the Wurlitzer family still in management.

Rolfing took over as vice-president and general manager while Rudolph H. Wurlitzer continued as chairman of the board and Farny R. Wurlitzer as president. Although it was a difficult time for everyone, the shift of authority and the reorganization was accomplished without much dissention. The company was changing from being a family business, and old sentimental relationships and loyalties had to be abandoned.

Farny Wurlitzer said that he and R.C. Rolfing never had a serious disagreement over the twenty years they worked together. They seemed to truly like and respect each other and focused on the rehabilitation of the business.

However, there was sharp disagreement over the fate of the North Tonawanda plant. The auditors and bankers urged that the plant be closed and sold. It had been operated as the Rudolph Wurlitzer Manufacturing Company, a wholly owned subsidiary. It was here that many of the Wurlitzer production triumphs had occurred, including the theater organ business. Farny strongly opposed the shuttering of the plant, taking the stance of a fighter, a rare position for him to take.

Farny argued that the financial losses could not be stopped by merely locking the plant's doors. If the property were to remain as an asset for future use or a saleable property, it would be necessary to keep a maintenance crew just to keep the buildings in shape. Farny estimated that those costs would be about $90,000 a year; if the buildings were abandoned, losses would be much greater.

Besides, the economic situation as it existed in 1934 would not have brought a fair price for the buildings in the foreseeable future. Rolfing agreed with Farny, and the decision was made to keep the plant in operation.

Rolfing came to the conclusion that Wurlitzer management should stay in its traditional field of music, so he decided to take Wurlitzer out of the refrigerator, furniture and radio businesses. He and Farny believed there was still a future in the piano business, in the limited production of organs and in the coin-operated automatic phonograph. Within a few weeks, Rolfing liquidated the inventories of radios, refrigerators and furniture at the North Tonawanda plant.

The board of directors continued to meet in Cincinnati, where Rolfing reported that the business continued to show red ink. Farny and Rolfing were on constant lookout for manufacturing and sales opportunities that would fit the Wurlitzer tradition. In March 1933, a year before Rolfing came into management of the company, a man named Homer Capehart wrote a letter to Farny, asking if Wurlitzer would be interested in buying manufacturing rights to a phonograph record changer for home use from the Packard Manufacturing Company of Fort Wayne, Indiana. Farny expected the return of saloons after the death of Prohibition, so he responded that rather than for home use, he would be very interested in a record changer to be used with coin-operated phonographs.

Ten days later, Capehart responded with circulars about a coin-operated device with record changer made in Chicago by the Simplex Phonograph

Jukebox developer Homer C. Capehart (with cigar) and two other Wurlitzer officials. *Courtesy of North Tonawanda History Museum.*

Corporation. And Capehart held the option to sell the Simplex business. Wurlitzer bought Simplex on May 27, 1933, and hired Capehart to manage sales. This new product, the automatic phonograph or jukebox, would prove to be very profitable as time went on. In 1933, 266 units were sold; by 1938, sales had soared to 45,092 units. Sales dropped dramatically in the shadow of World War II but rebounded after the war.

By 1937, the Rudolph Wurlitzer Company was well on the road back to prosperity. The unprofitable stores of the Depression were now profitable, and family differences had been resolved. Sylvia's son Eugene Farny was no longer with the company; his brother, Cyril Farny, had resigned from the board of directors but still managed the DeKalb, Illinois plant. Howard's son, Raimund, left the company at the time of his father's resignation, and Rudolph H.'s son, Rembert, resigned from the board but continued to handle the rare violin business. And Rolfing liquidated more than three thousand acres of real estate owned by the company that had been purchased by Rudolph H. By 1938, the period of transition was over and success was in the air.

From 1938, the Rudolph Wurlitzer Company made steady progress. Management placed increasing emphasis on research and innovation and adopted an aggressive sales policy. However, the coin-operated automatic phonograph industry ran into trouble shortly after World War II because of overexpansion and overselling. High inventory meant that automatic phonograph production at North Tonawanda was suspended in 1948. Although he was fantastically successful as a salesman, Homer Capehart left Wurlitzer in 1939 and was elected to Congress as a senator from Indiana, where he took an active role. Capehart was an ardent opponent of communism and many people believed that he supported Joseph McCarthy.

Sales of Wurlitzer pianos were relatively stable with heartening increases each year. In 1938, 9,874 pianos were made at the DeKalb factory. By 1942, that number had risen to 21,451. Piano manufacturing slackened during the war but returned to its previous level of growth afterward.

The electronic organ went on the market in January 1947, and the company focused research on producing a small, compact organ for home use. In 1953, Wurlitzer introduced the "Spinette" piano to great success.

Cyril Farny, Sylvia's son, resigned from the board of directors in 1937 but remained vice-president and manager of the DeKalb Division of the Wurlitzer Company. *Courtesy of North Tonawanda History Museum.*

Homer Earl Capehart, United States senator from Indiana, 1945–63. *Courtesy U.S. Senate Historical Office.*

A publicity photograph of Farny Wurlitzer, probably from the early 1950s. *Courtesy of Jeff Weiler.*

In 1941, Farny R. Wurlitzer became chairman of the executive committee of the board of directors, and Rolfing became president. This same year, the company's principal offices moved from 121 East Fourth Street in Cincinnati to 105 West Adams Street, Chicago. After fifty years with the company, Chairman Rudolph H. Wurlitzer resigned in 1943 and was succeeded by Farny as chairman; Rolfing continued as president.

All Wurlitzer production was now for support of the war, and its last pipe organ had been produced in 1942. The North Tonawanda plant developed and produced the flying bomb, the Bat. Wurlitzer emerged from the war in good financial condition and reconverted the plants to peacetime use.

By 1948, sales had again passed an all-time high with phonographs and auxiliary equipment accounting for half the sales figures; pianos, electronic organs, accordions and miscellaneous musical instruments accounting for 45 percent; and real estate operations accounting for 5 percent. However, sales of automatic phonographs brought surprising losses. Rembert R. Wurlitzer, vice-president and manager of the rare violin department, had resigned to enter the rare violin business on his own.

In 1950, Wurlitzer was well in the black, making television cabinets for television manufacturers, spinet and grand pianos, electronic organs and jukeboxes. In 1952, Wurlitzer introduced the Model 1500 jukebox that could play both 45- and 78-rpm records, the first of its kind. Wurlitzer sold its New York office building at 120 West Forty-second Street and adopted an employee savings and profit-sharing plan, as well as a continued compensation plan.

The North Tonawanda plant was hit with a general strike on June 11, 1954, the union demanding reinstatement of a union officer fired for sleeping on the job. The strike ended on August 17 without the employee being reinstated. Also in 1954, the company introduced a new jukebox, the Wurlitzer Carousel, that could play 104 selections from 45-rpm records.

The original DeKalb, Illinois plant was built in 1902 and, by 1955, had had about ten major additions, employing about 550 persons in the plant and 110 additional persons in the office and sales force. By contrast, the North Tonawanda facility employed 2,880 in the factory and 335 in the office in 1954.

R.C. Rolfing and Farny Wurlitzer at the August 1956 picnic in celebration of the company's centennial. The picnic was held on the lawn in front of the North Tonawanda factory. *Courtesy of North Tonawanda History Museum.*

As of May 1955, the Wurlitzer organization's executive office was located at 105 West Adams Street in Chicago, headed by President Rolfing. Farny R. Wurlitzer maintained his office in North Tonawanda. The DeKalb Divison was headed by James Rolfing, son of the president. James Rolfing died in 1961 in a tragic airplane accident along with several other Wurlitzer employees.

In 1956, the Wurlitzer Company celebrated its centennial. A new plant was opened that year in Corinth, Mississippi, to produce electronic pianos, electronic organs and, beginning in 1960, the Side Man drum machine. Also in 1960, the company opened a subsidiary, Deutsche Wurlitzer, in Hüllhorst, West Germany, to produce jukeboxes and electronic organs for the European and Middle Eastern markets.

Other European subsidiaries were established for the purpose of sales and distribution of Wurlitzer products. Wurlitzer Overseas AG was a Swiss corporation with offices in Zug, Switzerland; Wurlitzer Limited was established in 1964 in Winslow/Cheshire, England; and Wurlitzer Italia, S.r.l. began in 1967 in Livorno, Italy.

In 1961, another plant was opened in Holly Springs, Mississippi, to supply piano keys and actions to the Corinth and DeKalb factories. On April 5, 1965, Wurlitzer purchased the assets and factory of the Martin Band Instrument Company of Elkhart, Indiana. The first Wurlitzer-built Martin instruments were shipped from the factory in July 1965. In 1970, yet another plant was opened in Logan, Utah, to produce and supply the West Coast with acoustic and electronic pianos. In 1972, a second European plant was opened in Levern, West Germany. The two German factories produced coin-operated phonographs, cigarette and merchandise vending machines, electronic organs and electronic pianos.

Chairman of the Board R.C. Rolfing died in 1974, having served the Wurlitzer Company for forty years. Chairman Emeritus Farny Wurlitzer had died two years earlier. Even though the company reported record-breaking sales and earnings in its 1978 annual report, the loss of these long-term management leaders, combined with the economic recession of the early 1980s and declines in the piano and organ markets due to demographic changes in the United States, spelled the beginning of the end of the Wurlitzer organization.

Wurlitzer's 1986 annual report contained this ominous statement by the auditor, Deloitte, Haskins and Sells:

> *The Company is experiencing severe liquidity problems. At March 31, 1986, the Company's borrowings exceeded borrowing limits under its*

*secured revolving credit agreement and was in violation of several of the covenants of the agreement. The Company anticipates a net loss from continuing operations for the June 30, 1986 quarter in excess of $1.4 million. These continued losses are expected to reduce or eliminate the Company's margin of compliance under the modified credit agreement covenants. These factors, among others, indicate that the Company may be unable to continue as a going concern.*

In 1985, the Wurlitzer Company sold subsidiary Deutsche Wurlitzer to the Nelson Group, a privately owned organization based in Australia. Shortly after, the Baldwin Piano and Organ Company of Loveland, Ohio (in suburban Cincinnati), purchased the Wurlitzer Company. The company had been struggling for years because of foreign competition, high interest rates and a weak economy. The new electronic keyboard industry, which was dominated by Japanese companies, also played a role in the company's decline. After Wurlitzer was bought by Baldwin Piano and Organ, it stopped producing musical instruments and began making other wooden products such as billiard tables. However, Baldwin did continue to produce pianos under the Wurlitzer name for a time. In 2001, Baldwin Piano and Organ was bought by the Gibson Guitar Corporation, a company based in Nashville, Tennessee. Five years later, Gibson also bought Deutsche Wurlitzer from the Nelson Group. Deutsche Wurlitzer, still headquartered in Hüllhorst, discontinued the production of jukeboxes in September 2013 but remains a leading manufacturer of vending machines. There is a certain "full-circle" irony in the fact that Rudolph Wurlitzer emigrated from Germany to America in the nineteenth century and started a firm in the United States whose production returned to Germany in the twentieth century, where it continues today to bear his name.

# 9

# THE WURLITZER FACTORIES

Many businesses have served their country during times of war, and the Wurlitzer Company was no exception. Before the company was ten years old, it was making or importing and selling bugles and drums used by Union forces in the Civil War. During the years of peace following the war, Wurlitzer continued to provide bugles and drums for the government, as well as providing instruments used in the Spanish-American War.

The trumpets and bugles apparently were imported from France and Germany, but the Rudolph Wurlitzer Company made the drums in its own plant in Cincinnati. Howard wrote to his father on May 24, 1898, "We have now shipped the government 350 trumpets and 97 drums. We can turn out about 75 to 100 drums a week. The other contract for drums has not yet been given out, but if we should get it, I will employ more men so we can make about 200 drums a week." He told his father that he was two weeks ahead of the promised date on the drum contract.

In 1919, Wurlitzer purchased the distinguished Melville Clark Piano Company of DeKalb, Illinois, and began to produce pianos under the Wurlitzer brand. This was a significant event in the company's history. Until now, Wurlitzer had been primarily an importer of musical instruments; with the acquisition of the DeKalb factory, Wurlitzer was now also an exporter of musical instruments. From 1919 to 1973, the plant manufactured Wurlitzer pianos; from 1932 to 1948, accordions were also produced at the DeKalb facility. Unionized piano and accordion tuners at the plant went on strike on January 13, 1941, possibly as a result of Wurlitzer's effort to produce

Wurlitzer's DeKalb, Illinois musical instrument factory as shown in the company's centennial publication, *Wurlitzer World of Music, 1856–1956: 100 Years of Musical Achievement.* The factory was acquired by Wurlitzer in 1919.

Wurlitzer's Corinth, Mississippi piano factory opened in 1956, the year of the company's centennial. *From* Wurlitzer World of Music, 1856–1956: 100 Years of Musical Achievement.

an electronic tuner, threatening to make their jobs obsolete. The tuners were fired but were rehired and given back pay because of a ruling by the National Labor Relations Board in January 1942. In addition to producing pianos and other musical instruments, the DeKalb facility also built home stereo radio phonographs beginning in 1968. The *DeKalb Daily Chronicle* announced the final closure of the plant and the relocation of the company headquarters to Houston on February 27, 1987.

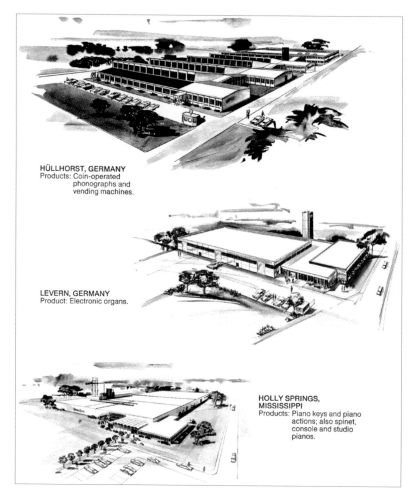

HÜLLHORST, GERMANY
Products: Coin-operated
phonographs and
vending machines.

LEVERN, GERMANY
Product: Electronic organs.

HOLLY SPRINGS,
MISSISSIPPI
Products: Piano keys and piano
actions; also spinet,
console and studio
pianos.

Wurlitzer's annual report for 1972 showed its factories in Hullhörst and Levern, West Germany, and Holly Springs, Mississippi.

Wurlitzer's centennial year, 1956, marked the opening of a new plant in Corinth, Mississippi, to manufacture electronic pianos, which had just been developed and were in high demand. Beginning in 1960, the plant also manufactured the new Side Man electronic drum machine.

Also in 1960, Deutsche Wurlitzer, a subsidiary, opened a factory in Hüllhorst, West Germany, to produce jukeboxes and electronic organs for the European market. In 1961, another plant was opened in Holly Springs, Mississippi, to supply piano keys and actions to the Corinth and DeKalb factories.

Wurlitzer's factory in Logan, Utah, opened in 1972. *From the Wurlitzer Company's 1972 annual report.*

On April 5, 1965, Wurlitzer purchased the assets and factory of the Martin Band Instrument Company of Elkhart, Indiana. The first Wurlitzer-built Martin instruments were shipped from the factory in July 1965. However, the Elkhart plant was closed in 1970, and the same year, a new Wurlitzer factory was opened in Logan, Utah, to produce and supply the West Coast with a wide variety of acoustic and electronic pianos. In 1972, a second European plant was opened in Levern, West Germany. The two German factories produced coin-operated phonographs, cigarette and merchandise vending machines, electronic organs and electronic pianos. In 1986, the German factories were sold to an Australian investment firm.

Of all the Wurlitzer manufacturing facilities, the factory at North Tonawanda, New York, was the flagship. The Wurlitzer building, located at 908 Niagara Falls Boulevard in the Martinsville neighborhood, started out as part of the booming carousel industry in North Tonawanda. Carousels were manufactured there by the Armitage Herschell Company beginning in the 1870s. The carousels needed barrel organs to provide music. The Herschell Company bought the barrel organs mostly from Europe through their European agent Eugene DeKleist but decided to start manufacturing their own to avoid ever-increasing import taxes.

The North Tonawanda Barrel Organ Company was formed in 1893, its first factory built at the current site of the Wurlitzer building. After Eugene DeKleist arrived from Germany to run the company, the firm became the DeKleist Musical Instrument Manufacturing Company and produced barrel organs, hurdy-gurdies, flute organs and military band organs.

Postcard view of the entrance to the North Tonawanda factory about 1916. *Courtesy of Gert Almind.*

Wurlitzer's North Tonawanda, New York factory about 1912. *Courtesy of Gert Almind.*

In 1908, Wurlitzer bought the company from DeKleist and renamed it the Rudolph Wurlitzer Manufacturing Company. Farny Wurlitzer was tapped to run the new factory and set about expanding the manufacturing complex. Two years later, Wurlitzer acquired the Hope-Jones Organ Company of Elmira, New York. This allowed Wurlitzer to expand to build both barrel and pipe organs.

The building is typical of industrial structures built in the early part of the twentieth century. By 1924, an iconic tower had been built to house a sixty-thousand-gallon water tank for reserve in case of fire. The modern portions of the building were constructed of reinforced concrete that not only made the building stronger and more versatile but also helped to reduce the risk of fire damage and allowed for larger windows.

Wurlitzer employees gather for a savings bond rally during World War I. *Courtesy of Regional History Center, Northern Illinois University.*

During World War I, Wurlitzer made bugles for the armed forces in a small plant in Chicago. At the same time, in the North Tonawanda plant, Wurlitzer curtailed its manufacture of pipe organs, player pianos and automatic musical instruments so that the facility could be devoted to the manufacture of boxes for 75-millimeter shells and packing cases for ammunition fuses. North Tonawanda was one of the great lumber markets of the country, and its workers had the needed woodworking skills. Using about five hundred employees, Wurlitzer made the shell boxes of yellow pine and the fuse boxes of poplar, with each fuse nested in a separate container.

By the end of World War I, the North Tonawanda factory was producing band instruments, band organs, calliopes, harps and upright and coin-operated pianos, along with automatic instruments, such as PianOrchestras and Paganini Solo Violin Pianos. With the entry of Robert Hope-Jones into the company and the production of pipe organs, the factory was expanded to provide space for assembly and shipping, a complete woodworking and finishing operation, a machine shop, an electrical and wiring department,

Postcard view of Wurlitzer's expanded North Tonawanda factory around 1926. *Courtesy of Gert Almind.*

offices and the five-story tower. An outdoor fishpond with adorning gateways and gardens completed the impressive approach to the building.

The advent of the talking movie spelled the demise of the pipe organ in theaters, and the Great Depression ended the building of new theaters. People turned to the inexpensive entertainment of the home radio in the early 1930s, so Wurlitzer turned its huge manufacturing facility and workforce to the production of home and portable radios under the name Lyric. Unfortunately, many other companies were doing the same, and the company fell on difficult financial times. Wurlitzer was brought out of its financial doldrums with a successful new product, the automatic phonograph, later called the jukebox.

During World War II, the company's manufacturing role was quite different. In addition to woodworking, between the wars, Wurlitzer had developed many skilled technicians in the fields of electronics and metalworking. Almost overnight, the manufacture of jukeboxes, pianos, organs, accordions and other instruments ceased. The plants at North Tonawanda and DeKalb were converted quickly to production of items needed for the war effort. The DeKalb plant won contracts for the production of guided missiles and leased an additional furniture factory nearby for this purpose.

The North Tonawanda factory produced wood glider parts, navigational magnetic aircraft compasses, wind-driven proximity bomb fuses, identification ("friend or foe") electronic radios, de-icing equipment for airplane wings and miscellaneous electronic and mechanical subassemblies for Bell Aircraft Company.

A company flier showed war production activities at the DeKalb plant in March 1945. *Courtesy of North Tonawanda History Museum.*

The DeKalb division's experimental work for the navy actually began in the summer of 1941, several weeks before the Japanese attack on Pearl Harbor. The factory adapted techniques in working with wood to the production of advanced types of naval aircraft and aircraft components. At the same time, the North Tonawanda plant was engaging in experimental research. The plant produced specialized and highly secret items for such companies as Bell Aircraft, Curtiss-Wright and Bendix Aviation.

The company's war effort was awarded the prestigious Army-Navy "E" Production Award. The North Tonawanda plant received the award in 1943 with two subsequent awards in 1944. The DeKalb plant received the award in 1944 with a subsequent award in 1945. Wurlitzer records show that, at the time, there were more than 3,000 persons on the payroll. Of that number, 584 had served or were serving in the military. When the war ended, Wurlitzer continued to research and manufacture military items for the U.S. government.

Around 1947, the U.S. Bureau of Standards awarded a top-secret contract to the North Tonawanda plant to research and develop a battery with an infinite shelf life but short-term active life. The battery was to be used to power a device to control proximity mortar shells and bombs. By 1950, the project had become a reality, and Wurlitzer was chosen to produce the RB46 battery. During the Korean War, Wurlitzer manufactured fifty thousand batteries per day. Twenty years later, this technology was declassified, and Wurlitzer further developed the battery technology for use in pacemakers. The technology later was sold to Medtronic, a medical technology firm, and is used for cardiac, brain and other nerve controls.

With the purchase of the Everett Organ Company near the end of World War II, Wurlitzer produced electronic home and entertainment organs based on the Everett "Orgatron" at North Tonawanda. Wurlitzer also began to produce jukeboxes again after the war and expanded its facility to over 750,000 square feet, mostly devoted to woodworking and the electronic organ business. The quality of Wurlitzer woodworking attracted television manufacturers Sylvania and Stromberg-Carlson, which contracted with the firm for the fabrication of wood TV cabinets.

In the mid-1950s, a labor strike lasting fourteen weeks signaled to management that they needed to look elsewhere for a manufacturing location. A new plant was then opened in Corinth, Mississippi. The electronic organ business became second in the United States, with production divided between North Tonawanda and Corinth. The military manufacturing arm of Wurlitzer produced mine detectors and radio receivers and undertook classified development work. It also developed musical products for merchandising by private label companies, including General Electric.

The North Tonawanda plant pioneered the creation of the modern jukebox in 1934, but their production gradually declined. By the 1970s, only jukeboxes and electronic organs were being made in North Tonawanda.

An advertisement from the 1950s for the Wurlitzer Spinette electronic organ shows the reed used in tone production.

Jukebox production was phased out in 1974, and the company's employees, once numbering about 3,000, dwindled to about 450.

Following a fire in the North Tonawanda plant, management decided to move manufacturing to Corinth, Mississippi, and Logan, Utah. In 1975, all production ended at the North Tonawanda plant, and the remaining two hundred employees were laid off. The military unit was disbanded, and

The entrance to the North Tonawanda factory about 1945. *Wurlitzer Company Records, Archives Center, National Museum of American History, Smithsonian Institution.*

The Wurlitzer Building in North Tonawanda today. *Courtesy of Gert Almind.*

only corporate engineering and research remained in North Tonawanda. Early in 1976, all functions of corporate headquarters, finance, marketing, advertising, sales and corporate engineering were consolidated in one location in DeKalb, Illinois. The final closure of the North Tonawanda plant took place in August 1976.

In 1978, Bill Irr Sr., along with two partners, bought the North Tonawanda building of 750,000 square feet to house the showroom and offices for his plumbing, heating and air conditioning wholesale business. The main building with its tower was purchased from Irr by his son-in-law Tom Austen in 1992. Austen is in the process of repurposing the building for retail, warehousing, offices and light manufacturing, while retaining the historical integrity of the building itself. The 380,000-square-foot complex currently houses about forty businesses, from a dog-training facility to lawyers' offices and a medical billing company. About 350 people are employed at the complex today. The remaining part of the building is still owned by Irr, who uses it primarily for offices and warehousing.

# 10

# THE WURLITZER RETAIL STORES

The first location of the Rudolph Wurlitzer Company in 1856 was a warehouse space in a small room on the upper floor of the building at Fourth and Sycamore Streets in Cincinnati. In 1858, Wurlitzer moved to larger quarters on an upper floor at 123 Main Street. By the time his brother Anton joined him in 1862, Rudolph owned the entire building at 123 Main Street and began retail sale of musical instruments.

Cincinnati addresses were renumbered about 1895, so addresses before that time do not indicate address locations today. The first store at 123 Main Street and the next one at 115 Main Street were both located in the present-day block of Main Street between Third and Fourth Streets.

The second retail outlet was opened in Chicago at 82 Dearborn Street in 1865. The city directory for the following year gives the store owners' names as John Molter of Chicago and Rudolph Wurlitzer of Cincinnati and describes the business as "Importers, manufacturers, wholesale and retail dealers in musical merchandise, general agency for A. Krakauer & Co.'s pianos, B. Shoninger's melodeons, parlor organs, etc." In 1867, the store had moved to 111 Randolph Street. It is likely that this store was wiped out in the great Chicago Fire of 1871.

Nearly thirty years after the Chicago fire, according to the directory of 1899, the Rudolph Wurlitzer Company opened a store at 78 Monroe Street with William H. Austin as manager. By 1901, the store had moved to 241 Wabash Avenue with George M. Koch as manager. E.H. Uhl was shown as

Wurlitzer's 1906 catalogue showed the rebuilt headquarters at 117–21 East Fourth Street in Cincinnati. The inset shows their Chicago branch at 266 Wabash Avenue.

manager of the store the following year, the beginning of his long successful career in management for Wurlitzer.

It is difficult to determine from the few company records from the early years exactly when, how and in what order other stores were established. An auditor's statement dated July 11, 1910, refers to leaseholds (presumably stores) "in New York, Philadelphia, Chicago, Cincinnati, and elsewhere" and in small cities near Cincinnati, such as Lexington, Kentucky.

Wurlitzer's first store in New York City opened in 1908 on Thirty-second Street between Broadway and Fifth Avenue. In 1910, a store was opened at 1835 Chestnut Street in Philadelphia. A Cleveland store at 800 Huron Road and a store at 701 Main Street in Buffalo opened on May 1, 1911. There was also a store in Dayton, Ohio, at that time. At a board meeting in 1912, leases were approved for stores in Detroit; Providence, Rhode Island; and Newark; and additional space was allocated for the Columbus store.

Wurlitzer catalogues also indicate the increase in retail activities. The company's 1912 catalogue listed additional stores in St. Louis and Louisville. Between 1913 and 1916, the company had nineteen retail stores, adding stores in Milwaukee, Boston, Pittsburgh, Rochester, San Francisco and Syracuse.

The growth of the stores is likely due to the leadership of Howard, who, by 1912, was president of the company. That year, a "player piano library" was established at the Chicago store with five thousand rolls. During these years, the board discussed at length purchasing real estate in downtown

Wurlitzer's Los Angeles store at 816 South Broadway in the 1920s was as sumptuous as any of the movie palaces nearby. *Courtesy of Jeff Weiler and North Tonawanda History Museum.*

Cincinnati, influenced by the booming city, rumors of a new railroad station to be built and the expanding business of the company. In 1913, the first Detroit store opened at 26 Adams Avenue West. Wurlitzer bought the Robert L. Loud music stores in Buffalo in 1918. In 1921, Wurlitzer bought out the Byron Mauzey Music Company in San Francisco and also had a branch store in Oakland.

Beginning as early as 1914, Wurlitzer had a long-term retail sales policy to offer music lessons along with its sales of musical instruments, giving truth to the slogan, "Music for the Millions." The company catalogue of that year devoted considerable space to the availability of home study courses created by experts in their respective fields. Beginning around 1925, the company offered private lessons and by the mid-1950s offered, among others, a package plan that included an instrument and 104 lessons. Teachers were contracted with Wurlitzer to conduct the music lessons either in the store or in the home. Big bandleader Sammy Kaye, actress Shirley Temple and many others received their first music lessons through Wurlitzer. In 1926, the Wurlitzer store in Los Angeles created the Baby Orchestra of twenty children, none of whom were over six years of age.

The Los Angeles store opened in June 1922. The stores on the West Coast and many of the others were very successful, cashing in on a pent-up demand from World War I. The Los Angeles store sold mostly pianos, pipe organs, phonographs and records. Business was so good in Los Angeles that the company built its own thirteen-story building there in 1924. In 1927, Howard announced his intention to have one thousand Wurlitzer stores throughout the country. Within a few months, forty-three Wurlitzer stores were operating in Southern California and fifteen in northern California, nearly all of them within a twenty-five-mile radius of Los Angeles and San Francisco.

The rapid expansion created enormous personnel and other management problems, complicated by the fact that the stores began to sell refrigerators and other items not related to the normally successful music lines.

Howard's expansion plan proved to be a money-losing venture in light of the economic events that were soon to come. Of course, this is easy to say in hindsight, and the company's expansion was in line with trend of the times. Signs of trouble began to appear at the December 29, 1927 board meeting with discussion of trying to dispose of a ninety-nine-year lease on 615 Wabash Avenue in Chicago. However, at the May 1, 1928 board meeting after Howard had retired and the new chairman of the board was Rudolph H., the company bought property in Oakland for $250,000.

The Wurlitzer store in Rochester, New York, in the 1930s. *Courtesy of Jeff Weiler and North Tonawanda History Museum.*

Sales were booming at all of the branch stores, as well as at the home store in Cincinnati. Throughout these years, the building that the Wurlitzer headquarters and store occupied at 121 East Fourth Street, Cincinnati, was owned personally by Rudolph Wurlitzer and his heirs.

By the time R.C. Rolfing became general manager of the Rudolph Wurlitzer Company on May 10, 1934, he found that the Retail Stores Division was a painful money loser and within six months began to close the Wurlitzer stores that were not producing profits. On October 3, Rolfing announced that the Lyric Piano Company and Milner Music Company, both in Cincinnati, had been closed, as well as the Robert L. Loud store in Buffalo and the Wurlitzer store in Akron. There were now only twenty-five stores left. The entire West Coast operation was closed within two years, and by July 1936, there were twenty stores: Ashland, Kentucky; Buffalo; Chicago; Cincinnati; Cleveland; Columbus; Dayton; Detroit; Hamilton, Ohio; Louisville; Middletown, Ohio; Milwaukee; New York City; Philadelphia; Piqua, Ohio; Rochester, New York; St. Louis; Springfield, Ohio; Syracuse; and Youngstown, Ohio.

However, in 1937, stores were reopened in San Francisco, Los Angeles and Brooklyn. When the old Los Angeles store had been closed, the rare violin department was continued under the management of Faris M. Brown. In 1938, the Middletown, Ohio store was closed, followed the next year with the closure of stores in Louisville, Syracuse, Youngstown and San Francisco. The 1940 annual report lists only ten stores: Brooklyn, Buffalo, Chicago, Cincinnati, Cleveland, Columbus, Detroit, Los Angeles, New York and Philadelphia.

The low point occurred in 1948 with the closing of the Cleveland store, one of the oldest in the group, due to the inability to obtain a satisfactory lease. The New York building was sold, and the six stores remaining were the choice ones, all in cities with populations of 500,000 or more: Cincinnati, Chicago, New York, Buffalo, Detroit and Philadelphia, five of them in Wurlitzer-owned sites.

The Retail Stores Division staged a profitable reorganization, and a new policy of expansion began about 1950. Small branch stores were opened

The Cincinnati store in the 1940s. *Wurlitzer Company Records, Archives Center, National Museum of American History, Smithsonian Institution.*

within a few miles of a large dominant store, which would provide the management and most of the inventory. For example, the main Chicago store was located at 115 South Wabash Avenue; branches were established in 1950 at Sixty-fifth and Halstead Streets and in Montclair; in 1952 at Evergreen Park; and in 1953 in Hammond, Indiana.

New stores were steadily added, and by 1957, there were thirteen retail locations and a new Wurlitzer display on "Main Street" at Disneyland in Anaheim, California, which had just opened in the summer of 1955. Wurlitzer supplied all the pianos and organs for the park. The company's 1967 annual report listed twenty-seven retail locations; the next year there were thirty-four. Forty-five stores were listed in the annual report for 1974. These stores were located in Boston; Cincinnati; Columbus; Detroit; Indianapolis; Milwaukee; Minneapolis; Newark, New Jersey; New York City; Philadelphia; and Pittsburgh. The report specifically touted the new Wurlitzer store at Livingston Mall: "Livingston Mall is located at the center of New Jersey's 'population explosion'...booming, affluent Essex County...over 1,000,000 people. Customers shop in living room comfort in this enclosed mall shopping center containing 1,100,000 square feet of shopping space. The Wurlitzer store is located near other national retailers, such as Sears."

At its peak in 1975, Wurlitzer listed forty-nine stores in fifteen metropolitan areas: Boston, Buffalo, Chicago, Cincinnati, Columbus, Detroit, Indianapolis, Kansas City, Long Island, Milwaukee, Minneapolis, Newark, New York City and Philadelphia. This was a substantial number but far fewer than the one thousand stores Howard Wurlitzer had envisioned in 1927.

The 1977 annual report noted forty-two stores. By the time Wurlitzer moved its corporate headquarters from DeKalb, Illinois, to Houston, Texas, ten years later, no retail stores remained.

# 11
# AUTOMATIC MUSICAL INSTRUMENTS

During the early part of the twentieth century, the Rudolph Wurlitzer Company, with headquarters in Cincinnati and its main factory in North Tonawanda, New York, was involved in nearly every phase of the automatic music business. No other American manufacturer came close to Wurlitzer in the sheer number and variety of automatic musical instruments produced.

## Regina Music Box

Beginning in the 1880s, America became interested in music boxes, and Wurlitzer was quick to add these to its retail lines. The Regina Music Box Company of Rahway, New Jersey, made many kinds of music boxes, but the most popular were boxes that played using an interchangeable metal disc. Although this kind of music box was also being mass produced in Europe, Regina was the largest American manufacturer of music boxes, and they sold very well. In time, Wurlitzer became the largest single sales outlet for Regina.

In 1896, Wurlitzer persuaded Regina to equip some of its music boxes with coin slots, particularly its large twenty-seven-inch-diameter disc changer machine. These Orchestral Corona models would play the choice of one

Wurlitzer provided placards like this one to establishments to promote their automatic instruments. The placards measured about seven by eleven inches.

tune for a nickel. Wurlitzer's great success in selling Regina products gave the company insight in the potential for coin-operated music.

## Wurlitzer Tonophone

Wurlitzer entered the field of mechanical music in a big way in 1897 with its association with Eugene DeKleist in North Tonawanda, New York. DeKleist was a manufacturer of barrel organs for use in carousels and contacted Howard Wurlitzer offering to sell some of the trumpets DeKleist made for the organs. Howard placed a large order for the trumpets and encouraged DeKleist to develop and build a coin-operated piano. Two years later, the result was the Wurlitzer Tonophone, a piano that played automatically using pinned cylinders similar to the ones DeKleist was using for his carousel organs. The piano was electrically operated and of course had the coin-in-the-slot attachment. Two major styles were available, with keyboard and without. Most Tonophones sold were without keyboard, as the addition of a keyboard added $150 to the cost.

Wurlitzer ordered two hundred Tonophones. The instrument was a smash success as soon as it appeared on the market, providing music in cafés and other public establishments. Demand was so high that DeKleist had to upgrade his

The Wurlitzer Tonophone as depicted in the company's 1909 catalogue of automatic musical instruments. The Tonophone was operated by a large pinned cylinder, similar to a music box, and driven by an electric motor.

production methods to a production-line factory. The public liked the honky-tonk sound of coin pianos, and the Tonophone was manufactured from 1899 to about 1908. One disadvantage to the Tonophone, however, was the fact that new cylinders cost forty dollars each, a large sum at the time.

Within two years, Wurlitzer became the sole sales agent for DeKleist's products in the United States. The success of the Tonophone led to the development of other coin-operated machines: the Pianino, the Mandolin Quartette and the Mandolin Sextette, all produced at the DeKleist factory beginning in 1906. The latter instruments produced a mandolin-like repeating sound, along with piano accompaniment.

The business with Wurlitzer made DeKleist wealthy, yet he allowed his factory to languish from inattention, and the quality of the machines suffered. Howard Wurlitzer, as head of the Wurlitzer business, gave DeKleist an ultimatum: either sell the business to Wurlitzer or Wurlitzer would set up a factory elsewhere to make the machines themselves. DeKleist sold his business to Wurlitzer in 1908.

In 1906, Farny Wurlitzer took control of the automatic music department in the Cincinnati office. With the acquisition of the DeKleist factory in North Tonawanda and his management of it, Farny was able to not only sell automatic instruments with the Wurlitzer brand but to manufacture them, too.

## *Barrel and Band Organs*

Wurlitzer sold band organs made by DeKleist beginning in the late 1890s. With the purchase of the DeKleist Musical Instrument Manufacturing Company in 1908, Wurlitzer now produced these instruments instead of buying them at wholesale from DeKleist or importing them from German makers. An early Wurlitzer catalogue offered

> *Pinned Cylinder Military Band Organs, for merry-go-rounds, ballyhoo, tent shows, excursion steamers, and all sorts of out-of-door amusement resorts. For years our pinned cylinder organs have been recognized as the best the world affords. Built in the largest, most complete factory in the world, of the best materials money can secure, by skilled mechanics with a lifetime of experience in the business, they excel in tone, construction, mechanical simplicity, case design, arrangement of the music, and all the details necessary in a first class organ. The increasing demand for a first class pinned cylinder band organ has induced us to add several new styles with drums and cymbals.*

Wurlitzer converted many band organs of all makers to use Wurlitzer cylinders and, later, to use Wurlitzer paper rolls. The early band organs were made mainly for skating rink use. They had to be loud to be heard over the din of hundreds of wooden roller skate wheels on a wooden rink floor. Since loudness was one of the prime considerations, most of these had brass horns, drums and cymbals. Later, the organs were made for more general purposes, including not only skating rinks, but also for

In 1922, Wurlitzer marketed this Style 157 band organ to customers who wanted a fancy medium-sized instrument. This band organ is nearly eight and a half feet high and over twelve feet long. *From the Sanfilippo Collection. From* The Golden Age of Automatic Musical Instruments, *copyright 2001, Arthur A. Reblitz. Used with permission.*

amusement parks, traveling shows and so forth. Only a few of these later styles have brass horns. According to sales literature of the time, Wurlitzer band organs provided the "only correct music for skating rinks, fairs, carouselles and summer resorts."

Band organs reached their peak of popularity before World War I, but they remained very popular with some amusement operators long after other automatic instruments had gone out of style. Wurlitzer sold its last band organ in 1943.

## Wurlitzer Pianino

The forty-four-note Pianino was the first Wurlitzer coin piano to operate using a perforated paper roll and was introduced about 1902. The Pianino had an automatic rewinding device and tempo control. Each roll played for fifteen to twenty minutes and contained six musical pieces and made the

Pianino a bestseller for Wurlitzer. To provide a variation in the sound, each machine was equipped with a mandolin attachment. This device, a small slotted curtain with a row of metal buttons, produced a tinkly mandolin-like effect when it was lowered between the piano hammers and the strings.

Around 1910, the forty-four-note pianos began to go out of style, but Wurlitzer continued to produce them into the 1920s. Wurlitzer added additional sounds to the machine with the Violin Pianino, adding twenty-one violin pipes and twenty-one flute pipes. By the late 1920s, Violin Pianinos added xylophones as standard equipment.

The Wurlitzer Bijou Orchestra featured a forty-four-note piano with mandolin attachment, twenty-one violin pipes, twenty-one flute pipes, a xylophone and a snare drum. According to sales literature, the instrument was "designed to meet the demand for a small automatic orchestra suitable for any but very large public places. The 'Wonder Lamp' at top in the center is very attractive. It constantly revolves and changes colors when playing. The art glass designs vary somewhat." The Bijou Orchestra also contained an innovation: the Wurlitzer automatic roll changer, allowing six music rolls to be stored and played on the machine at one at a time.

## Wurlitzer Automatic Harp

In 1905, Howard Wurlitzer saw a self-playing harp in a downtown Cincinnati café and was impressed with its soft melodious tones. He decided it was just the thing to add to the Wurlitzer line.

The harp's manufacturer was J.W. Whitlock and Company of Rising Sun, Indiana, a small Ohio River city about thirty-five miles downstream from Cincinnati. Whitlock had made a few of these self-playing harps as an experiment and had put them on location in Cincinnati, the nearest large city. Wurlitzer quickly established an agreement with Whitlock to sell the harps on an exclusive basis. The two firms signed a contract for one thousand harps, and on the strength of this contract, J.W. Whitlock and Company constructed a new wooden building and set up production-line manufacturing facilities. The agreement placed a firm order for one thousand harps at $200 each, to be delivered in three years, at the rate of thirty-five per month.

The new machine was immediately reintroduced as the Wurlitzer Automatic Harp. An initial catalogue description read:

*After nine years of constant labor, at great expense, we have succeeded in perfecting the Wurlitzer Harp, a most refined musical instrument for places where the piano cannot be used on account of its being too loud.*

*This beautiful instrument is conceded by everyone who has seen and heard it to be the most wonderful as well as the sweetest musical instrument ever produced.*

*The harp contains sixty fingers (almost human in their operation), and produces a volume of soft, sweet music equal to several Italian harps played by hand. The face of the instrument is covered by a large harp-shaped plate glass, showing the interior lit up by electric lights and the wonderful little fingers picking the strings. This feature gives the instrument an exceedingly attractive appearance.*

*As a money-maker in fine hotels, cafés, restaurants, cigar and drug stores the harp has proven itself to be the King of them all; its soft, sweet music making it exceptionally popular in places where other instruments would be too loud.*

The inventor of the automatic harp was J.W. "Row" Whitlock (1871–1935), an entrepreneur and inventor who had successes not only with the automatic harp but also with furniture making and record-setting speedboats. In the 1890s, when Row was twenty, a childhood friend of his named Harry Connors was active playing harp at the hotels in Cincinnati. Connors would also spend time visiting Row at his home in Rising Sun. Connors and Whitlock reasoned that if one could make a self-playing harp, then Connors could leave them behind when he performed live at hotels and restaurants in Cincinnati.

Whitlock built seven harps and took six of them to Cincinnati to be exhibited. The initial showing of the harps was not very successful, most likely because of the lack of marketing expertise of the inventor. However, Cincinnati turned out to be the ideal place to try out the harps because it was there that the Rudolph Wurlitzer Company took notice of them. Wurlitzer offered the machines at $750 each, which was almost a 400 percent markup on the wholesale price and ten times the production cost.

On August 18, 1907, the 1,000th harp rolled off the assembly line of the Whitlock factory. The Rudolph Wurlitzer Company had executed the first of its options for another 500 harps, and production continued. The second batch was sold at $125 each to Wurlitzer, which still allowed $60 profit for Whitlock. The harp had clearly been a success for Wurlitzer.

The Wurlitzer Automatic Harp, Style A, as shown in the company's 1909 catalogue of automatic musical instruments.

Like other automatic instruments sold by Wurlitzer, the automatic harp was viewed as not only a source of beautiful music but also as a source of revenue for the owner of the restaurant that housed it. A 1906 Wurlitzer catalogue listed 135 business locations in Cincinnati that had an automatic harp that would begin playing at the drop of a nickel. The electric motor-driven mechanism used perforated paper rolls containing six selections each. When a roll reached the end, it automatically rewound within a few seconds and was then ready to repeat the program.

In 1909–10, demand for the harps slackened, and production rates declined. In November 1906, the new Style B had been introduced to help increase the harp's appeal. But Wurlitzer never exercised its option for another 500 harps to total the 2,000 originally envisioned. In fact, Wurlitzer canceled its order altogether near the end of the 1,500 harps committed.

The Style A automatic harp was placed in a rectangular oak case with a fancy fretwork surrounding plate glass cut in a harp-like shape. Style B automatic harps, introduced in 1906, were placed in cases "built on the lines of the original Italian harp," complete with column and harmonic curve. Styles A and B were virtually the same from a mechanical standpoint, and both were lit from within by an electric light.

The last automatic harp was produced in late 1910 or 1911. By 1916, they were being "remaindered" for $375 each, half their original selling price. Toward the end of the automatic harp's market life, Wurlitzer must have been trying to push the remainder anywhere it could. A book published in the 1930s entitled *The Barbary Coast: An Informal History of the San Francisco*

*Underworld* by Herbert Asbury alludes to the depths to which the automatic harp sank:

> *Each girl* [from the parlor houses] *had one day off a week, which she usually spent with her lover or drinking in the dives of the Barbary Coast. The parlor houses also derived a considerable income from the sale of beer in bottles—and for music. Practically every resort was equipped with some type of automatic musical instrument, usually electric, which played only when fed with nickels or quarters. A great deal of the revenue from the music and sale of liquor went to the police and politicians as graft, in addition to the regular payments which were usually based on the number of girls in a house.*
>
> *In the late spring of 1911, the police forbade all music in houses of prostitution and ordered the removal and destruction of every musical instrument in the red light district. A month later in July, the proprietors of the houses were told that they might provide music for the entertainment of their guests, but that it must be music of the Automatic Harp. There wasn't such an instrument to be found in the Barbary Coast* [the San Francisco red-light district], *but the lack was soon remedied. A few days after the house owners had been notified a salesman for a Cincinnati piano house appeared in the district and offered automatic harps for sale at $750 each. He bore references from important politicians and experienced no difficulty in making sales.*

Apparently, at least one Wurlitzer employee knew politicians in San Francisco who were obtaining revenue from the instruments as graft. Otherwise, why would the local authorities require automatic harps and other automatic instruments in bordellos?

The music that was arranged for the automatic harp numbered about 1,400 tunes. They varied from a few classical pieces to waltzes and marches, popular songs and character pieces arranged from piano music. Most prevalent, however, was ragtime, since the development of this instrument coincided with the growth of ragtime. Music rolls for John Philip Sousa's "Stars and Stripes Forever" appeared in June 1906 and were followed in July by Scott Joplin's "The Entertainer." Other popular music rolls included "Turkey in the Straw," the "Toreador Song" from Bizet's *Carmen* and "At a Georgia Camp Meeting."

Whitlock never intended his harp to play glissandos since it was set with sixty chromatic pitches in the center of the piano range with no overall sostenuto dampers or expression. Each "magic finger," or picker, had a damper that allowed music similar to the player piano arrangements popular at the time. In the original patent, the pickers were made of metal. A different picker made of wood was eventually used, to give the harp a softer sound.

Around 1,100 Style A harps were made. The change of case design to the Style B took place in 1906, and about 400 Style B harps were made.

## Wurlitzer Player Piano

In 1908, the first Wurlitzer sixty-five-note player piano was introduced, replacing the Tonophone as the standard large coin-operated piano. Like

The Wurlitzer Player Piano, as depicted in the 1909 company catalogue. This instrument used perforated rolls rather than a pinned cylinder as in the Tonophone.

the smaller Pianino, this new player piano used perforated paper music rolls instead of a pinned cylinder. The piano was produced in several hundred different styles and minor varieties; some were one-of-a-kind items made on special order.

Unlike other manufacturers, Wurlitzer music rolls were intended to be used in more than one type of machine that they produced. In 1925, ten different kinds of rolls were available; four of them could be used on more than one type of machine.

Also introduced in 1908 was the Wurlitzer Violin Piano, with the addition of a set of thirty-eight violin pipes placed behind the soundboard. Soon after, models were produced with drums and a triangle added. These were first sold as Wurlitzer Violin-Flute Pianos; later, the name was changed to the Wurlitzer Orchestra Piano.

Automatic instruments with expanded instrumentation such as this were now being called "orchestrions." Arthur Reblitz defines an orchestrion as "a self-contained automatic musical instrument, especially a large one, equipped with several different instruments in imitation of an orchestra, and usually containing some percussion effects (for example, snare drum, cymbal, triangle, etc.)."

With Wurlitzer's purchase of the Melville Clark Piano Company in DeKalb, Illinois, the company also began offering reproducing pianos under the Apollo brand. These pianos had the ability to play loudly and softly instead of at a single volume, as was provided by player pianos, and included control of the damping pedal, giving the instrument almost human-like expression.

## *Philipps Pianella and Wurlitzer PianOrchestra*

In 1903, the same year that the Wright brothers were experimenting with their airplane on the North Carolina coast, Wurlitzer introduced a large orchestrion, the PianOrchestra. From 1903 to 1914, Wurlitzer imported about one thousand of them from J.D. Philipps und Söhne in Germany, who had named them "Pianella." When Germany went to war in 1914, imports of these instruments were reduced, so Wurlitzer took on the task of making them at the factory in North Tonawanda. From about 1903 to 1920, PianOrchestras were made in dozens of styles and in hundreds of minor variations. Wurlitzer catalogues stated that no two were exactly alike, usually with variations in case ornamentation.

The huge instrument had 188 pipes imitating flute, piccolo, clarinet, violin and cello, a piano with mandolin attachment, xylophone, bells and an array of seven percussion effects.

About 1910, Philipps introduced a new type of instrument, the Paganini, made in over a dozen different models ranging from the basic instrument containing a reproducing piano plus violin pipes to the very large Paganini Violin Orchestra with several ranks of pipes plus bells, xylophone and percussion effects. The Paganini was intended to play serious and soulful piano and violin music. It is estimated that one or two hundred of these instruments were sold in America. Around 1913, Wurlitzer began manufacturing PianoOrchestras and Paganinis at North Tonawanda, importing some of the "guts" of the instruments from Philipps, with Wurlitzer providing the cases and the remaining inner workings.

A Wurlitzer Style C automatic piano was the simplest photoplayer for film accompaniment. This advertisement shows the side cabinet opened for viewing. *From* Encyclopedia of the American Theatre Organ, Vol. 3.

This advertisement from the September 5, 1914 issue of *Moving Picture World* is an example of Wurlitzer's philosophy of owner endorsements.

# Photoplayers

Around 1913, Wurlitzer entered the photoplayer market. Nickelodeon theaters were then common—storefront or other small theaters that showed silent films and charged five cents for admission. There was thus a large demand for music to accompany the silent films. Wurlitzer produced several styles of theater instruments, ranging from a basic piano with two ranks of pipes to larger styles with two side chests. The overall design of a photoplayer is wide and low, for use in the orchestra pit or just below the movie screen.

Wurlitzer sold these instruments as Theatre Orchestras, Motion Picture Orchestras or One Man Orchestras. The Wurlitzer Style K Pipe Organ Orchestra, one of the largest still in existence, contains a piano, 196 pipes, a xylophone, orchestra bells, chimes, drums and many sound effects, such as fire gong, auto horn, automobile exhaust, Chinese cymbal, bird whistle, cowbell, wind, waves, telegraph key, crackling flames and horse's hooves.

A photoplayer operator had to load and unload various music rolls throughout the showing of a film in order to match the action on screen; by pulling handles, pushing buttons and stepping on foot pedals, the operator could orchestrate the fast-changing movie scenes by providing march music, romantic interludes, funeral dirges or whatever the screen demanded.

In 1916, Wurlitzer advertised that "every day more than two million people listen to Wurlitzer music!" By 1928, the popularity of sound movies virtually ended the market for photoplayers and theater organs. The photoplayer business was completely over by 1930.

# 12

# THE MIGHTY WURLITZER

With the theatrical success of the photoplayer, which used pneumatic music rolls in addition to human operator action throughout the showing of a movie, it made sense for Wurlitzer to develop a theater instrument that was played entirely by a human, allowing for more musical expression. The result was the "Wurlitzer Hope-Jones Unit Orchestra," known today as the "Mighty Wurlitzer," and initially offered in 1910.

The genius behind the instrument was Robert Hope-Jones (1859–1914), a native of Cheshire, England. Hope-Jones experimented with the use of electricity to provide the connection with the organ's keyboard and the pipes at St. John the Evangelist Church in Birkenhead, England, where he was choirmaster and occasional organist, beginning about 1887. The application of electricity to organ actions had first been demonstrated in France in 1866, but by 1886, the idea had been nearly abandoned. Hope-Jones had a very creative mind with a background of musical and electrical interests, so he took up the challenge of designing electro-mechanical mechanisms. He installed them in the St. John's organ, where he controlled them from a console that could be moved to any location, including outside in the churchyard. Other church congregations noticed Hope-Jones's innovations and wanted electrically controlled organs installed in their own parishes. To meet the needs of organ builders, he established the Hope-Jones Electric Organ Company in Birkenhead to permit them to construct electric actions using his patented principles, eventually licensing them to some twenty organ-building firms. The licensing idea didn't fare very well since Hope-Jones's inventions had no lengthy track record and were not

Robert Hope-Jones in his thirties. *Courtesy of Jeff Weiler and North Tonawanda History Museum.*

fully perfected. Eventually, however, the Hope-Jones firm manufactured electrical components for the trade and, by 1894, began manufacturing complete organs.

For all his brilliance and inventive ability, Hope-Jones was a terrible businessman, a condition that typically affects genius. He never grasped the reality that a business needed to make a profit in order to survive. The Hope-Jones Electric Organ Company failed in 1897, so he allied himself with organ firms in Europe and the United States. These relationships were all unfavorable in the end.

Hope-Jones partnered with Eustice Ingram in Hereford, England, and established Ingram, Hope-Jones and Company. This relationship also soured. In April 1903, Hope-Jones was caught in a sexually compromising position with one of his workmen. His business partner Eustice Ingram initiated legal proceedings against Hope-Jones, resulting in him and his loyal wife, Cecil (pronounced seh-seal), taking the next boat to America, leaving all their belongings behind in England. Although an allegation of homosexual activity was considered to be very serious a century ago, Hope-Jones was charming and had a charismatic personality that inspired staunch loyalty. Many of his employees followed him from employer to employer both in England and the United States.

The Hope-Jones name was known in America, and he was soon hired by the Austin Organ Company, a relationship that lasted only six months. An ensuing failed partnership with Lewis C. Harrison, with whom he formed the Hope-Jones and Harrison Company, resulted in dissolution of the company in August 1905. Next, Hope-Jones joined the firm of Ernest M. Skinner as a vice-president. Both Skinner and Hope-Jones were egocentric and individualistic, and within fifteen months, Skinner fired Hope-Jones.

One of the organs that Hope-Jones worked on with Skinner was in the Park Church in Elmira, New York. He made a number of friends in the church whom he persuaded to help him establish the Hope-Jones Organ Company in 1907. One of the more famous investors in the new firm was Mark Twain. By 1908, the company had fifty-nine employees, and Hope-Jones was continuing to invent and perfect his organ mechanisms. However, he continued to engage in spending sprees that could not be controlled by the investors, and in late 1909, he was arrested for having sex with a young man at the factory. Although he was given a suspended sentence, the fine of $500 was too much for the investors to bear, and the company was bankrupt in early 1910.

At the same time, Wurlitzer was ramping up its manufacturing capacity in North Tonawanda, less than two hundred miles away from Elmira. The Hope-Jones Organ Company was bankrupt but didn't fail because of lack of business. When the doors were closed, the company had six organ contracts. Hope-Jones could not prevail on any of his eastern friends for additional funds, so he looked to the west and approached Wurlitzer to invest in the failed company.

Wurlitzer proposed that they not invest but rather buy the firm outright. The Wurlitzer brothers already understood and exploited the developing market for organs installed in secular locations, especially the "unit organ" in continuous development by Hope-Jones. Wurlitzer bought the firm in May 1910 for $15,800 and eventually hired Hope-Jones, realizing that they needed his guiding genius if the unit organ was to succeed. His contract prohibited him from using his name or talents to benefit any firm other than Wurlitzer.

The relationship between Hope-Jones and Wurlitzer proved to be extremely difficult. Hope-Jones had little understanding or desire to make the financial aspects of the business successful; the Wurlitzer Company looked at the financial bottom line constantly, to the detriment of Hope-Jones's creative genius. Each side viewed the other as without merit and inflexible.

In particular, Howard Wurlitzer, who was running the company from his office in Cincinnati, looked at the tiniest detail of everything and was a number cruncher who saw only the bottom line. He typically ignored the feelings of his associates, seeing individuals as expendable and ignoring their emotional needs. Hope-Jones, on the other hand, was egocentric, had intense charisma and was a persuasive salesman in addition to being an inventive genius.

Farny Wurlitzer, in charge of the North Tonawanda facility, still had to receive approval from his brother in Cincinnati in nearly all business decisions. Farny was more humane and people oriented than his iron-fisted eldest brother, Howard, but even he ran into difficulties with Hope-Jones. It is remarkable that the relationship between Hope-Jones and Wurlitzer lasted as long as it did—four years.

In addition to organizing the factory and training new employees, Wurlitzer expected Hope-Jones to design a group of stock Unit Orchestras with self-player attachments. They saw the profit potential in instruments that could be mass produced instead of custom made. The stock instruments that he designed were Styles 3, 6, J, L and M. However, Hope-Jones continued to refine and tweak the design, creating friction with his superiors at Wurlitzer. Farny wrote several memos complaining to Hope-Jones of his practice of changing the design of an instrument without first discussing it with Farny regarding the financial implications. Hope-Jones fired back that he was sure that Wurlitzer didn't want to "clip his wings" but rather wanted to allow him to provide the company with the best service he could. He needed to be a free agent and held a grudge when his ideas were not met with enthusiastic acceptance.

Because of Wurlitzer's success with automatic instruments, the company wanted the stock Unit Orchestras to have self-playing mechanisms. Although Hope-Jones wasn't especially thrilled with the idea, he responded to the challenge of designing a player mechanism. In the early years, Wurlitzer's attitude toward organists was one of disdain and toleration. Everyone was expected to be subservient to the company as a whole. After all, assembly-line workers could easily be replaced. Unfortunately, this approach didn't work very well in the arts. The company alienated several prominent musicians who could have demonstrated the Unit Orchestras. These musicians spread the word among their colleagues, resulting in Wurlitzer's loss of church, residence and concert hall business that could have been theirs with the value of Hope-Jones's name.

While Wurlitzer's treatment of its own employees was worse than its treatment of the organists, it was no different than any other company's treatment of workers of the day. There was a marked difference in the way Hope-Jones treated his employees: he treated them with respect and supported higher wages and raises for worthy employees. This was moving too far in the other direction from Howard Wurlitzer's approach. On several occasions, Hope-Jones asked to be released from his employment contract, but fearing the advantage a competitor would have with the Hope-Jones name, Wurlitzer refused to let him go.

When Wurlitzer bought the Hope-Jones business, it was more interested in the creation of an instrument that could substitute for an entire orchestra than it was in creating organs as such. The most difficult disagreement Wurlitzer and Hope-Jones had was over the use of the Hope-Jones name versus the Wurlitzer name. Hope-Jones insisted that his product be called the Hope-Jones Unit Orchestra; the company insisted that its name be used to name the product Wurlitzer Unit Orchestra. Later, Farny allowed that the instruments could be called Wurlitzer Hope-Jones Unit Orchestra. The company discovered that the term "unit orchestra" could not be copyrighted; however, "Wurlitzer" and "Hope-Jones" were registered commercial trademarks, both owned by the Wurlitzer Company. But each would have preferred that the other's name be excluded from the instrument's name.

Although Hope-Jones complained often about his inadequate compensation (sixty dollars per week), it was nearly three times that of the highest-paid factory employee. In the spring of 1914, Farny had reached his limit and banned Hope-Jones from the factory. He was expected to work from his home in Buffalo.

Instead of staying in the Buffalo area near the North Tonawanda factory, Hope-Jones moved to New York City and took up residence in the Hotel McAlpin. Wurlitzer demanded that he return to Buffalo. Hope-Jones requested one hundred dollars to defray the cost of returning to Buffalo, which was eventually advanced to him. But Hope-Jones was spiraling downward, making unreasonable demands on his employer.

Seeing no further opportunities in New York City or elsewhere, and having alienated his employer, on September 13, 1914, Robert Hope-Jones committed suicide, having devised a unique method worthy of an inventor. He taped a rubber tube to his mouth and attached the other end to a gas jet. To a tee in the tube he attached a burner, which he lit. After his death, the ignited burner prevented escaping gas from harming anyone else nearby. He is buried in Buffalo's Elmlawn Cemetery, and his loyal and devoted widow, Cecil, was provided for with a 1 percent commission on organ sales from Wurlitzer, as stipulated in his employment contract.

Much as Wurlitzer might have wanted, it discovered that it couldn't limit production of the theater organs to stock instruments; custom-built instruments were also needed. The instruments had to be assembled and tested at the factory and then dismantled and shipped to the final location for final installation on site. It was not possible to hire qualified workers from elsewhere in the country. It was more practical to hire local people and train them with wages substantial enough that they wouldn't be hired away by competing firms. In 1919, the North Tonawanda factory had about seven hundred employees, 13 percent of whom were employed in the Unit Orchestra department.

In 1910, only one Unit Orchestra was shipped; by 1919, seventy-one were shipped, mostly stock instruments. The Style 3 was the smallest of the stock organs, with two manuals and seven ranks of pipes. It was replaced by Style 185 in 1918. The Style 40, with three ranks of pipes and a straight-rail console, was built in 1918 but was so unpopular that only one was made. Style J had two manuals with four ranks of pipes with piano console (i.e., piano-like straight-line keyboard) and was superseded by the Style 1 in 1916 and the Style 135 in 1918. Additional piano console models were the Styles N and V in 1915 and the Style 110 in 1919. Style 110 was the smallest, with three ranks of pipes; Style V was the largest with eight ranks.

Larger models with a horseshoe-shaped console were also introduced. The Style 4 had two manuals and eight ranks of pipes; Style 35 was a three-manual, fifteen-rank instrument, and Style 4 was the largest regular model without a Tibia Clausa stop. Style 5 had two manuals and nine ranks, but only one was built before being replaced by Style 210 in 1919.

On most other Wurlitzer products, traditional serial numbers were assigned and stamped on the instrument during manufacture. This was not the case for pipe organs, band organs and harps, which had their numbers assigned just before shipment. The Unit Orchestras are referred to today by "opus" number, referring to the sequence of an instrument's manufacture. Wurlitzer never used this numbering system, and it does not appear in any original Wurlitzer records, yet it has been brought into common usage by historians who were probably influenced by other organ manufacturers who used the term "opus."

A few weeks after Hope-Jones's death, Farny Wurlitzer was asked by a Denver theater owner, Samuel L. Baxter, to create an instrument for his Isis Theatre that would be larger and more impressive than the three-manual, fourteen-rank Wurlitzer in the Paris Theatre up the street in order to attract Paris customers to the Isis. Farny gladly rose to the occasion with the installation of a four-manual, twenty-eight-rank organ costing $40,000. The instrument, built in 1915 and now designated Opus 64, included a piano played from the organ and sound effects, such as xylophone, harp, chime, wind, rain, thunder and lightning. The Isis Theatre Wurlitzer was a resounding success. As part of the sales agreement, Wurlitzer agreed to not install another larger theater organ in Denver for five years.

Many of Wurlitzer's theater organs were moved from the buildings where they were originally installed to other locations. An example of this

A four-manual, thirty-four-rank theater organ is being tuned in the Wuritzer factory erecting room prior to being dismantled and crated for shipment to the Fisher Theatre in Detroit. *Courtesy of Jeff Weiler.*

is the organ currently in Plattsburgh, New York. The instrument, Opus 970, was originally installed in the New Olney Theatre in Philadelphia in 1924. In 1964, it was moved to the home of Leonard and Louise Johns in Hingham, Massachusetts. The Johnses donated the organ to the Strand Theatre in Plattsburgh in 2004. It was restored and installed in the Strand by the Spencer Organ Company of Waltham, Massachusetts, in 2012. It boasts three manuals and eight ranks of pipes, with xylophone, glockenspiel, cathedral chimes and a variety of percussion effects.

There are other examples of relocated instruments in Cincinnati. Opus 1680 was originally installed in the 3,500-seat RKO Albee Theatre downtown in 1927 at a cost of $55,000. With the Albee slated for demolition, the instrument was relocated in 1968 to the Emery Theatre, once the home of the Cincinnati Symphony Orchestra. At the Emery, it was used for concerts before and after sound movies and to accompany silent pictures. The Emery closed in 1999, and the organ was dismantled once again, with

Ron Wehmeier at the console of the restored RKO Albee Theatre organ relocated to the ballroom of Music Hall, Cincinnati. In the background is the Steinway grand piano connected to the organ console. The remaining organ pipes and other effects are located behind the filigreed screen. *Courtesy of Philip Groshong.*

the component parts stored in a warehouse and other locations, including the homes of the members of the Ohio Valley Chapter of the American Theatre Organ Society.

The organ's new owner, the Ohio Valley Chapter, vowed to keep the instrument intact if at all possible and reinstall it somewhere downtown. A new home was found in the Music Hall ballroom, and an anonymous donor offered a gift of $1.41 million to fund the repairs and installation. Ron Wehmeier, a well-known area organ technician, was hired to relocate and reinstall the instrument. The newly refurbished organ had its dedication concert on November 28, 2009, with Ron Rhode at the console. The organ has three manuals and thirty-one ranks of pipes. Additional features include a Steinway grand piano and a variety of percussion and other special effects from fire gong to klaxon and police whistle.

Wehmeier has also installed a large Wurlitzer theater organ in his home just a short distance from downtown Cincinnati. He acquired an instrument from organ collector Russ Nelson and enlarged it to thirty-seven ranks, constructing a special room to house it. The console is from the Wurlitzer

The music room in the home of Ron Wehmeier in Cincinnati. In addition to a Wurlitzer theater organ, the room houses several pianos and a Wurlitzer harp. *Courtesy of Philip Groshong.*

originally built in 1926 for the Southtown Theatre in Chicago. His additions to the instrument include portions of the 1922 organ built for the Circle Theatre in Indianapolis. Wehmeier's music room also includes several pianos and a Wurlitzer harp.

Wurlitzer organ sales saw a significant increase in 1920, with the all-time peak of production taking place in 1926. The North Tonawanda factory had been enlarged several times, and 1,113 people were employed. Wurlitzer had been the industry leader, selling twice as many theater organs as its nearest competitor, the Robert Morton Organ Company. Wurlitzer had gotten in on the ground floor of the theater organ business and created a demand for instruments where there had been no demand before. Since Wurlitzer had been in business for more than fifty years before selling its first pipe organ and with the exposure of its retail stores and its automatic instruments in so many public places, the advertising slogan "the name that means music to millions" was not just hyperbole.

With the introduction of the sound motion picture, combined with the effects of the Great Depression, demand for the Mighty Wurlitzer slackened. From 1933 to 1943, only fifty opus numbers for new instruments were made. The final Unit Orchestra shipped from the factory was a rebuild of Opus 1118, shipped on October 27, 1943. Wurlitzer had made 2,234 Unit Orchestras and had installed them in venues large and small all over the world.

## *Residence and Player Organs*

Automatic instruments were a mainstay of the Wurlitzer Company beginning in 1909, and demand for automatic instruments carried over into the theater organ business such that, through 1922, about 40 percent of Wurlitzer pipe organs were equipped with player mechanisms. By 1926, only 1 percent had player mechanisms.

Private homes were a valuable market for player pipe organs. In the days before high-fidelity sound reproduction, reproducing pianos and pipe organs were the only real option for enjoying fine music in the home. Unfortunately for Wurlitzer, the Aeolian Company had a near monopoly on the residential market. From 1911 to 1925, Wurlitzer sold only eighteen organs to residence customers, less than 2 percent of the company's pipe organ business.

In 1924, the Style R player was created, controlling a three-manual organ and ninety-two stops. A new line of residence organs was introduced in 1926, ranging in size from the Style R5 with two manuals and six ranks of pipes to the R25, with three manuals and fourteen ranks. The prices were higher than charged by other makers, so in 1928, Wurlitzer introduced the RJ series (for "junior"), designed to appeal to buyers with a limited budget. These organs were smaller, with three to seven ranks, and some models omitted percussion effects.

With the market for theater organs in sharp decline after the advent of talking movies, Wurlitzer was quite aggressive in promoting residence business through extensive advertising in national magazines. Wurlitzer sold twenty-three RJ organs to homes and funeral parlors and ten Series R organs to wealthier customers. Despite the smaller market share, Wurlitzer produced some 2,200 residence and player organs.

Beginning in the 1950s, theater organs enjoyed a renaissance, with private individuals acquiring instruments from theaters and installing them in their homes. It is interesting to note that the number of theater organs reinstalled in homes was several times the number sold by the factory for that purpose.

# Entertaining is a rare delight with a
## WURLITZER REPRODUCING ORGAN

THERE'S a lull in the conversation. Then, an expectant hush, as you touch an electric button; and instantly, your guests are listening enraptured to the glorious harmonies with which your Wurlitzer Reproducing Residence Organ floods your home. Symphonies, ballads, classical or popular selections as you will, all are rendered with that

brilliant blending of countless tone colors, that soul-stirring grandeur which make the pipe organ the acknowledged "King of Musical Instruments." For entertainment on all occasions, the Wurlitzer residence pipe organ, played either by hand or by reproducing music rolls, and requiring surprisingly small space, brings you the world's best in music. There is no

measuring the value of the pleasure it gives your guests and your family, the cultural development it affords your children, the distinction it adds to your home. Yet the cost is only about half what you would expect to pay for so wondrous an instrument. You are invited to hear and play it at the nearest Wurlitzer Studio—New York, Buffalo, Cleveland, Cincinnati, Detroit, Los Angeles, Chicago.

This advertisement for the Wurlitzer Residence Reproducing Organ appeared in the July 1929 issue of *Country Life*.

# Church Organs

Since Wurlitzer had unwittingly excluded itself from the church organ business because of its cavalier treatment of influential organists, the company's market share was much smaller for church installations. Whereas the marketing of theater instruments catered to the theater owner who viewed the instrument as a necessity, along with seats, screen and ticket booth, church organ customers were more discerning. The artistic or musical merit of an instrument was very important to a church; the normal techniques used by Wurlitzer to sell an instrument to a theater owner did not work in a church setting.

Nevertheless, Wurlitzer sold organs to 256 religious institutions. Most had two manuals with less than eight ranks. Instruments moved from other locations (including theaters) constituted a fifth of all church sales. Wurlitzer had to sell the church organs at about half of what it charged for theater instruments in order to compete with prices charged by other manufacturers.

The Wurlitzer name had become synonymous with secular music, a fact that deterred many prospective church customers. However, a few were drawn to Wurlitzer because of the notoriety of the name. When screen star Mary Pickford selected an organ to donate to the Church of the Good Shepherd in Beverly Hills, California, in 1924, it was a Wurlitzer. When she was asked why she picked a Wurlitzer, she responded innocently, "Is there any other kind of organ?"

Wurlitzer designed a series of stock models called "schemes" rather than the term "style" as used for their theater and residence instruments. At least two dozen models were produced, from the Scheme 5 with two manuals and three ranks to Scheme 90 with three manuals and eleven ranks. The choice of the word "scheme" was unfortunate indeed for Wurlitzer. Imagine a salesman attempting to sell a church a *scheme*!

In 1930, Wurlitzer introduced its least expensive series of instruments, the Chapel Models, in a last-ditch attempt to gain a larger portion of the church market. By the end of the decade, traditional Wurlitzer church organ production had ended.

# 13

# PIANOS AND HARPS

## *Pianos*

The first Wurlitzer piano was manufactured in Cincinnati in 1880, and by 1890, the company carried "a full line" of upright and square pianos. According to the *Pierce Piano Atlas*, between 1903 and 2001, over 2.8 million pianos carrying the Wurlitzer name were produced, primarily at its factories in DeKalb, Illinois; North Tonawanda, New York; and Corinth, Mississippi. The instruments produced at these factories after 1937 all carried the trademark "Wurlitzer." Before 1937, other trade names that were used included Apollo, Julius Bauer and Company, Melville Clark, DeKalb, Farny, Kingston, Student Butterfly Clavichord, Kurtzmann, Merriam, Schaff Brothers, Spinette Strad and Underwood. In 1985, Wurlitzer bought the Chickering brand, and ten years later, Wurlitzer was purchased by the Baldwin Piano and Organ Company of suburban Cincinnati. Baldwin had Wurlitzer grand pianos built by Young Chang in South Korea until about 1996, when production was moved to the Samick Musical Instrument Company's factory located in Indonesia. Gibson Guitar Corporation acquired the Wurlitzer name in 2001, when it purchased Baldwin Piano and Organ Company.

Sales literature from 1910 lists fourteen different piano models, such as the Style 805 Studio Upright ("half the size and weight of an ordinary upright"), the Farny Upright Style 642, the Farny Player Piano Style 710, the Apollo Reproducing Upright Style 709R and six different grand pianos from the four-

**Six and Thirty Black Slaves ~ Two and Fifty White**

Eighty-eight slaves are yours to command —notes on the piano keyboard—slaves waiting to bring you the collective treasure of the great composers of all times.

The piano is an integral part of modern homes, because those who appreciate beautiful surroundings also appreciate music . . . . . those who play on a Wurlitzer know the added pleasure of a perfect medium of expression.

Rich in outward appearance, the Wurlitzer Small Upright is in perfect harmony with modern living room surroundings.

Less in size than the standard upright, this remarkable little instrument fits into the smallest room . . . . . yet has the resonant golden tone, the beauty of line and finish which make Wurlitzer pianos distinctive.

**WURLITZER**

| WURLITZER | Upright Piano Factory | Grand Piano Factory |
| Small Upright | NORTH TONAWANDA, N. Y. | DE KALB, ILLINOIS |

WURLITZER, North Tonawanda, N. Y.        DEALERS AND BRANCHES EVERYWHERE
*Upright Treasure Chest of Music.*

Please send me your free booklet "Childhood and Music" and brochure of Wurlitzer Small Upright Pianos.

Name_____

Address_____

City _____ State_____

N. T.-BH3                    © 1928 Wurlitzer

This piano advertisement from 1928 appeared in *Better Homes and Gardens.*

foot, nine-inch-long Studio Grand Style D to the seven-foot W Parlor Concert Grand Style D4.

In 1919, Wurlitzer purchased the distinguished Melville Clark Piano Company of DeKalb, Illinois. From 1919 to its closing in 1973, the plant manufactured Wurlitzer pianos. Common practice in the piano industry was to use trade names on pianos whose designers and makers had long since gone out of business. In 1935, there were forty piano manufacturers in the United States, yet the instruments carried over 300 brand names. This same year, Wurlitzer rejected this marketing method. An internal memo from circa 1950 titled "Confidence Assured in Wurlitzer 'One Name' Policy" described Wurlitzer's approach to branding its pianos:

*Those who visit the* [DeKalb] *plant and see modern piano production developed to its highest degree of efficiency, can't help but notice that every instrument made here bears the name "Wurlitzer." In all national advertising, too, the name, "Wurlitzer" is proudly identified with all products made by Wurlitzer. There is only "one name" and that name is "Wurlitzer," the same name which appears on the factory, the identical name which marks the main entrance, the exact name featured in all national advertising, and the only name used on Wurlitzer instruments. Wurlitzer does not employ second, stencil or ghost names because it is the belief of Wurlitzer that such a practice would be confusing to the customer, to the salesman and to the dealer.*

The Wurlitzer Butterfly Grand piano was introduced in the mid-1930s and was an instant success. *Wurlitzer Company Records, Archives Center, National Museum of American History, Smithsonian Institution.*

Wurlitzer never intended its pianos to compete with those of higher-end manufacturers and instead focused on the durability and overall quality of the instruments. Wurlitzer was the first American piano company to offer to the middle-class, urban American public a well-made, good-sounding, sturdy but small (even portable) piano that could fit in a smaller space, like

153

a midtown city apartment. In 1935, Wurlitzer took the American piano market by storm with the Spinette, a piano with a full-sized keyboard and a full set of strings, yet standing a mere thirty-nine inches high. Also in the mid-1930s, Wurlitzer introduced the Butterfly Grand, a small instrument with a top that was hinged in the center, allowing its "wings" to be opened from each side. It was an instant success. In 1994, Wurlitzer reissued the instrument in an electronic version.

Wurlitzer pianos made during the twentieth century were considered to be "workhorse" instruments, similar to those made by the Kimball Company or Cable Company. These pianos were not in the same league as the Steinways, Mason and Hamlins or Chickerings and were not marketed as such. Wurlitzer's goal was to have a grand piano, a baby grand piano,

The most recent Wurlitzer pianos offered by Baldwin included this C173 ebony grand. *Courtesy of Gibson Guitar Corporation.*

an upright, a studio or a spinet in every living room of every home in the United States. Professional musicians and students would be using other, better-built pianos to perform on, but they would likely find a Wurlitzer in a practice room or at a cocktail party. Wurlitzer pianos have stood their ground over the years. After the company's sale to Baldwin in the late 1980s, the name was still respected enough for use on certain lines.

Wurlitzer pianos had several exclusive features like the "calibrated element," which was an extension of the lower end of the treble bridge so as to move as many notes as possible toward the center of the soundboard. Another feature was the "hexagonal soundboard" that extended the soundboard up farther into the bass area of the smaller pin block. Wurlitzer claimed that this innovation added 11 percent more surface area to the soundboard.

In 1948, Wurlitzer offered pianos with "plastic fabric finishes," such as the Model 425, in addition to traditional wood finishes. The introduction of the durable (but optional) "Wur-Lon" finish for Models 315 and 2155, in addition to traditional wood finishes, came in 1955. Wur-Lon was advertised as a "wear resistant finish" that was water- and stain proof, scratch resistant and impervious to temperature changes.

Over the years, Wurlitzer bought out smaller piano manufacturers, such as Cincinnati's Smith and Miller Piano Company in 1909 and, in 1985, Aeolian Pianos of Memphis, Tennessee. Even after the Wurlitzer Company was sold, Wurlitzer-branded acoustic pianos continued to be available until 2008.

## Electronic Pianos

Wurlitzer marketed its first Model 100 electronic piano in 1954 and in 1956 began the manufacture of organs and electronic pianos in its new plant in Corinth, Mississippi. In 1961, the company's new plant in Holly Springs, Mississippi, was devoted to the manufacture of piano keys and actions for Wurlitzer instruments, as well as producing keys and actions to the specifications of other manufacturers. In 1970, the manufacture of pianos and electronic pianos began at the new Wurlitzer plant in Logan, Utah.

Sales literature for the new electronic piano stated that the piano was:

*Ideally suited for small living quarters—light weight gives it portability for convenient playing or easy storing wherever used—delightful musical qualities blend perfectly as accompanying instrument or stand out impressively as solo instrument (making it highly desirable to any musical group as well as professional entertainers)—embodies such unique features as ear phones and volume control creating an instrument perfectly suited for classroom and studio training—holds special appeal for children, making it an excellent instrument to start a child's musical education. There is no limit to the versatility of the Wurlitzer electronic piano.*

Most of the Series 100 electronic piano cabinets were made of a fiberboard-composition wood-like material with a speckled finish. Colors ranged from beige and a pinkish-tan to mint green and a glossy black. The instrument concealed a built-in amplifier with vacuum tubes in early models but later used a solid-state amplifier. By 1968, the pianos were offered with colorful vinyl tops in a choice of deep red, dark green, tan or basic black. The Wurlitzer electric piano was a sixty-four-note instrument with a range of an octave above the lowest pitch of a standard eighty-eight-key piano to the C an octave below the top pitch of an eighty-eight-key piano. The tone was produced from a single steel reed for each key, activated by a miniature version of a conventional grand piano action and forming part of an electrostatic pickup system. The piano also had a sostenuto pedal similar to a conventional piano. By the 1970s, these pianos were commonly used not only in rock and jazz bands but also in educational institutions. The Wurlitzer Music Laboratory had a base teacher's instrument with up to forty-eight student instruments. Using headphones, each student as well as the teacher could listen to only their own piano or any combination of the others. A microphone allowed the teacher to address each student individually or as a group. Wurlitzer officials grandly estimated that 75 percent of all universities used the Wurlitzer Music Laboratory. The last model of Wurlitzer electronic piano was made in 1984. Although the market was quickly overtaken by other manufacturers, some Wurlitzer classroom piano laboratories were still in operation as late as 2000.

## Wurlitzer Harps

Rudolph Wurlitzer was said to be "passionately fond of the harp and its music," and for many years, the company had been importing European harps made by Erard, Erat, Dodd, Grosjean and others. These harps were sold through the general catalogue. Repairs made on these imported harps at the Cincinnati store made it obvious that there was a need for a harp that could better withstand the American climate and the demands of contemporary music. The first harps made by Wurlitzer at its Chicago factory appeared in 1909 and were made under the direction of Emil O. Starke (born 1863), who had worked with George B. Durkee at the Lyon and Healy harp factory in Chicago for twenty years.

The early harps manufactured by Wurlitzer made only a few departures from the European models. Among the innovations mentioned in the 1909 Wurlitzer general catalogue were mechanical parts all made by machine with all fittings removable and interchangeable, using standard screw threads. The pedal mechanism, or "action," that controlled the use of flats and sharps was "free from any questionable innovations, and the general plans of the immortal Erard" were followed. The harps used pivot-bearing and cone-bearing spindles, and the only springs used were in the pedals themselves. The pedal rod runways were bushed with piano felt, the column then said to be "solid." Early Wurlitzer harps were offered in three styles: I, II and III.

Soon after he began working at Wurlitzer, Starke made several important modifications in the design of his harps, and he changed to alphabetic model-name designations. The new Wurlitzer harps were sturdier than the European harps and carried the designation "Starke Model" on the brass action plate. The body ribs were made of maple, and the Wurlitzer harp had a patented anchor and shoulder brace, patented by Wurlitzer in 1911, that minimized the need for frequent regulation of the harp action. Mechanical precision was improved, and the action mechanism was enclosed between the brass plates of the neck. The pedal rods were enclosed in individual brass tubes within the column, making the pedal movement much easier and less noisy. In the Wurlitzer harp, the pedal rods were changed to a parallel arrangement, making them less susceptible to breakage. The soundboard was strengthened by covering the usual single-cross grain with a veneer of vertical grain. On the larger model harps, the soundboard was extended to exceed the width of the body of the instrument at its lower end, where the heavier strings needed greater amplification. The pedals were wrapped in leather, and rubber shoes could be purchased to cover the pedal tips.

The Wurlitzer harp was awarded a medal of excellence at the 1915 Panama-Pacific Exposition in San Francisco. Endorsements soon followed by conductors Walter Damrosch, Fritz Reiner and Leopold Stokowski, as well as by European harpists Anton Zamara, Luigi Maurizio Tedeschi, Marcel Grandjany; American harpist Harriet A. Shaw of Boston; and many

A publicity postcard of Luigi Maurizio Tedeschi and his Wurlitzer harp. The inscription reads, "The Wurlitzer is the best harp in the world." *Wurlitzer Company Records, Archives Center, National Museum of American History, Smithsonian Institution.*

others. An especially elaborate harp was made in 1914 for the Italian-born harp virtuoso Alberto Salvi.

Both the Wurlitzer harps and the harps made by competitor Lyon and Healy had much stronger wooden frames than harps made previously. The harmonic curve of the harps consisted of several ply thicknesses of maple, perpendicularly laminated. Both makers veneered their harp bodies in fancy maple. Brass action plates and pedals were used, the disc action was gold plated, string pins were nickel plated and so on. Although the harps were produced in factories, they were still the product of skilled craftsmen who gave each harp individual attention. Above all, the tone of each instrument was the primary concern of both the harp maker and the harpist.

According to Wurlitzer sales literature of 1924, the Wurlitzer harp claimed "pre-eminent superiority of tone over any other harp." The tone was said to be of greater volume, also rounder, thicker and of a richer quality because of the use of ribs or braces of maple rather than of metal. Vigorous playing of fortissimo passages never resulted in the disagreeable "twang" common to other makes of harps. The Wurlitzer harp had longer string length than other harps of comparable size. And because of the patented anchor and shoulder brace, "no regulation even in the slightest degree has ever been found necessary" by the professional harpists who endorsed the Wurlitzer harp.

In fact, these improvements seem to have made the Wurlitzer harp *too* responsive, and in their 1924 catalogue, the Wurlitzer Harp Tone Damper was announced:

> *The need of a practical and effective pedal damper that would relieve the hands of that function has always been felt by harpists. Harp makers have vied with each other to produce a damper which would be noiseless and sure in its action. Musical effects are obtained by our invention which will add very much to the success of concert and ensemble performers. The vibration of the strings may now be controlled instantly at will, by means of an extra pedal to be operated by either foot. This latest invention puts the harp where it rightfully belongs, on an equal with the piano.*

The damper was endorsed by Henry J. Williams, solo harpist with the Minneapolis Symphony Orchestra, and was patented by Wurlitzer in 1927. Apparently, few instruments with the damper pedal feature were produced, as examples of it are extremely rare.

In 1931, Starke patented a new bracing plan that consisted of a tailpiece made of metal "within the acoustic chamber for anchoring the strings of a

This photograph from March 1929 shows a worker installing the action mechanism on a Style GG Wurlitzer harp. *Courtesy of Louis Rosa.*

A worker at the Wurlitzer harp factory prepares a harp body to receive its soundboard in this photograph from March 1929. *Courtesy of Louis Rosa.*

harp." It is likely that Starke had retired by this time, accounting for the fact that the patent was not assigned to Wurlitzer.

While Wurlitzer's success in producing a superior harp was an enormous prestige factor in the music world of the time, its harp factory was never profitable. In the mid-1920s, production was moved to the North Tonawanda facility. Wurlitzer continued to make harps there until 1934, when production ceased.

The Rudolph Wurlitzer Company made harps through serial number 1560 between the years 1909 and 1933. This represented only two-tenths of 1 percent of overall Wurlitzer production (piano production during this time accounted for nearly one-half of all items manufactured by the company). Most Wurlitzer products were assigned a traditional serial number during manufacture. This was not the case with the harps, whose serial numbers were assigned just before shipment.

Since no surviving harps have a serial number below 500, it is likely that the numbering system

Wurlitzer harp Style I "Small Orchestra Special" from the 1924 harp catalogue. *Courtesy of Regional History Center, Northern Illinois University.*

started with 501. Between 1921 and the late 1920s, the following styles were made: A, B, C, I, DX, DD, CC, AX, CCX, AA, DDX-D, Special GG-G and Special DD. Although information is incomplete, the firm apparently changed back to numerical model designations in the late 1920s, possibly to be more consistent with Lyon and Healy's numerical style designations. Wurlitzer's

This introductory page from Wurlitzer's 1924 harp catalogue shows an unidentified harpist playing a Style CC harp. *Courtesy of Regional History Center, Northern Illinois University.*

Style 20, which proved to be very popular, first appeared in 1928. Wurlitzer also made Styles 5, 10, 25 and 30. Styles 25 and 30 had forty-seven strings and an extended soundboard. Style 25 was seventy-three inches tall; Style 30 was seventy-two inches in height. The weight of the Starke Model Wurlitzer harps ranged from sixty to eighty pounds.

Models with a single letter style name referred to a straight soundboard instrument; double letters referred to one with an extended soundboard. The harps were finished in metal and either smooth or stippled gold leaf or both. Sales literature particularly stressed that no plaster of Paris or other moldings were used in decoration. The middle section of the column was in natural finish, with only the fluting gilded. The soundboards were decorated with a decalcomania floral design and a gold stripe. Harps made before the early 1920s had a different design on the soundboard. An X suffix on the style name referred to a Gothic design such as the DDX. The body of the harp was made of curly maple, and the enlarged soundboard had a beechwood bridge.

Although Wurlitzer made harps for only twenty-five years, harpists around the world still recognize the innovations in their design, the richness of sound and the quality craftsmanship that was used in their manufacturing.

Wurlitzer Style DDX Gothic design harp from the 1924 harp catalogue. *Courtesy of Regional History Center, Northern Illinois University.*

# 14

# JUKEBOXES

Most historians agree that the term "jukebox" comes from the word *jook*, originating in the western part of Africa and brought to the United States by black slaves. *Jook* means to dance or act wildly or disorderly. These workers gathered in "jukes" or "juke-joints," places where they socialized after a long day in the cotton fields of the American South. Associated with such places of rowdiness was the "jukebox," an inexpensive way of providing lively dance music.

In order to avoid unsavory association with such low-class entertainment, Wurlitzer preferred to call them "automatic phonographs," but in a few years, public usage forced the acceptance of the term "jukebox." According to Ken Mountain, by 1942, Wurlitzer had produced an astounding 450,000 jukeboxes, with overall Wurlitzer production eventually estimated at more than 5 million units.

Wurlitzer's first jukebox was the ten-selection Debutante, released in 1933, which used the Simplex mechanism of record handling, a technology that Farny Wurlitzer had bought from Homer Capehart. That, coupled with a coin-in-the-slot mechanism similar to that used by Wurlitzer in its automatic musical instruments of the previous era, promised to be a successful product when marketed to the owners of restaurants, taverns and other public places. Farny hired highly skilled professionals for design and marketing. Over the next few years, Wurlitzer jukeboxes became widely embraced by operators, and by the late 1930s, Wurlitzer was producing over forty-five thousand jukeboxes a year. The jukebox became known as the "small man's concert hall."

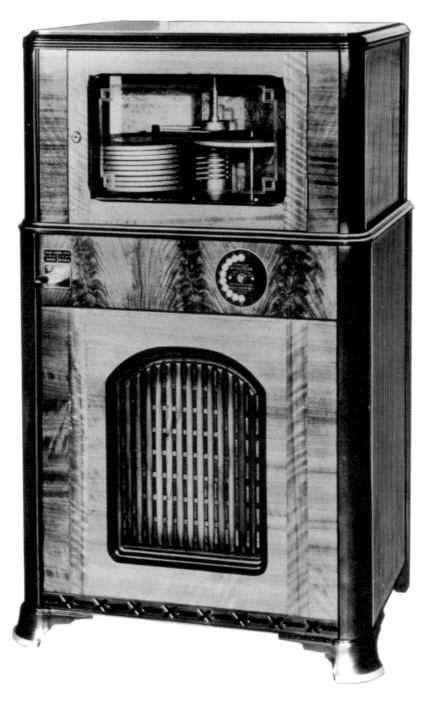

Wurlitzer's first jukebox, the Debutante model of 1933. *Courtesy of North Tonawanda History Museum.*

A Model 616A jukebox prepared for shipping in 1939. *Courtesy of Gert Almind.*

By the beginning of World War II, the jukebox had become such an integral part of American life that Glenn Miller recorded a hit pop song, "Jukebox Saturday Night," and in 1942, Hollywood made a movie featuring the jukebox. It was titled *Juke Girl* and starred a young actor named Ronald Reagan as an itinerant fruit picker in Florida who falls in love with co-star Ann Sheridan, who plays a hostess in a seedy dance hall.

The machines were built too well to fall apart and thus did not encourage annual replacement; sales soon leveled off. Wurlitzer dealt with this problem by establishing a unique trade-in policy, offering a twenty-five- to fifty-dollar credit toward one of its new models to any operator who traded in any make or model jukebox. Wurlitzer then destroyed the old jukebox.

In addition to floor-model jukeboxes, the early years of production of Wurlitzer machines included countertop models, usually providing twelve selections and intended as an inexpensive alternative to a full-size machine for smaller venues. The components were mechanical, with a stack of records from which the patron made his choice before inserting a nickel. When the

166

## WURLITZER SMALL MODEL PHONOGRAPHS

**A COUNTER MODEL FOR THE LOCATION HAVING NO AVAILABLE FLOOR SPACE**

### *The Model* 61 ... SPECIFICATIONS

Height 22", Width 21¼", Depth 18", Weight 115 lbs. Amplifier, Model 841. Tubes—1 type 79, 1 type 80, 2 type 41. Output 6 watts. Volume Control, Key Type, Lighting Wattage 47½. Total wattage 140. Tone control 3 step—low, medium, high. Finish: quilted maple and California walnut with ebony finish base. Illuminated plastic corners. Coin Equipment: One 5 cent slide. Plays 12 records.

### *The Model* 51 ... SPECIFICATIONS

Height 20", Width 27½", Depth 18½", Weight 120 lbs. Speaker 8" Dust-Proofed, Dynamic Amplifier, Model 741, four tubes, 1 type 79, 1 type 80, 2 type 41; Output 7 watts—Volume Control: Keytype level, compensated—Pickup Magnetic—Total Instrument Wattage, 110—Tone Control, 3 step; low, medium, high. Cabinet, figured African Mahogany matched veneers, Acacia Burl inlays and ebonized bands. Record Compartment Back, variegated colors on fluted background. Ebonized Baseboard. Plays 12 records.

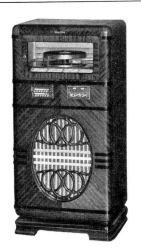

### *The Model* 50

•

### SPECIFICATIONS

•

**A CONSOLE MODEL**
*for*
**THE LOCATION HAVING RESTRICTED FLOOR SPACE**

Height 47½" with casters. Width 23¼", Depth 17¾", Weight 165 lbs. Amplifier Model 752, 5 tubes, one type 76, one type 6A6, two type 2A3, one type 80. Output 12 watts. Speaker 10" Dust-Proofed Dynamic. Volume Control: Keytype, level compensated. Total Instrument Wattage, 165 watts. Pickup Magnetic. Tone Control, 3 step; low, medium, high on amplifier. Cabinet, figured African Mahogany matched veneers. Record Compartment Back, variegated colors on fluted background. Ebonized Baseboard. Grille, handsomely carved and brilliantly lighted with "Lucite" bars. Plays 12 records.

Wurlitzer also produced countertop jukeboxes as shown in this advertisement from 1938. *Courtesy of North Tonawanda History Museum.*

coin rolled down the chute, the entire stack of discs moved up or down until the selection reached the tone arm. Then rods or posts with washers lifted the entire pile of records above the selection, leaving room for the tone arm to slide over and play the chosen tune.

Jukebox production replaced organ pipe production at the North Tonawanda factory. This photograph from circa 1939 shows workers assembling sixteen-selection jukebox mechanisms. *Courtesy of Jeff Weiler.*

The competition among the major jukebox manufacturers was fierce. Wurlitzer soon found itself among the "big four" jukebox manufacturers: Seeburg, Rock-Ola and AMI (Automatic Musical Instrument Company, acquired in 1962 by a company now known as Rowe International). Wurlitzer's early machines were rather stodgy in appearance and resembled the floor-model radios of the period. In order to increase their visual appeal, in 1935, Wurlitzer hired a gifted designer, Paul Fuller (1897–1951). A native of Switzerland, Fuller had immigrated to the United States in 1920 and went to Chicago to work for the firm Marshall Field and Company, where he soon became the chief designer in charge of interior decorating. In the '30s, he was the originator, designer and principal owner of the popular Black Forest village display at the Chicago World's Fair (1933–34) and also designer of the Sun Valley alpine village at the New York World's Fair (1939–40). As soon as he was hired by Wurlitzer, he started to explore alternatives to the conservative wood-and-glass jukebox cabinet styles.

Paul Fuller (center) poses in 1937 with his newest design, Model 616A, with a speaker grille that incorporated Lucite in a jukebox for the first time. Joining Fuller are (left) Carl E. Johnson, plant manager for the North Tonawanda factory, and (right) Raymond C. Haimbaugh, director of engineering at North Tonawanda. Both of these men later served on Wurlitzer's board of directors. *Courtesy of Gert Almind.*

Fuller's Model 24 of 1938 was the first to feature the use of electric lights and plastic. It also offered an expanded selection of twenty-four tunes, advertised as "the broadest selection ever offered in any automatic phonograph." In fact, Capehart declared it as the ultimate selection: "That's all the music we'll ever

The K-600 jukebox (with keyboard selector) was featured at the 1939 New York World's Fair. *Courtesy of Regional History Center, Northern Illinois University.*

need on a jukebox," he remarked. By 1947, competitor Seeburg was using its new record changer with the ability to play both sides of each of fifty records, effectively offering one hundred selections. Seeburg's new machine also featured a window to reveal the changer mechanism for the first time, a design element that had always been common to Wurlitzer jukeboxes.

Fuller's use of color, moving lights, Catalin plastic and bubble tubes (described then as "liquid fire"), provided the flash and style sought by Wurlitzer. The bubble tubes were a product of Biolite, Inc. of New York City, and were being used in advertising signs. The tubes were first used in the Wurlitzer Model 800 jukebox.

The 1940s are known as the "golden age" of the jukebox, and Fuller designed new models in the early 1940s, such as Models 700, 750 and 850. With their sophisticated and artistic use of plastics, glass and wood, Fuller's designs became instant classics, establishing Wurlitzer as a formidable force in the industry. Fuller went on to design seventeen jukeboxes for Wurlitzer before he resigned from the company in late 1948 because of ill health.

With America's entry into World War II in 1941, the use of metal and plastics was curtailed, so Fuller responded with the Model 42 Victory and the Model 950, both of which relied heavily on the use of wood and glass.

The most iconic of the Fuller designs was the Model 1015 jukebox, introduced at the end of the war in 1946. Its styling details included animated bubble tubes, revolving lighted color columns and a revealed record-changing mechanism. The 1015 sold over fifty-six thousand units during its first eighteen months on the market and eventually became the most successful jukebox of all time. Fuller's final Wurlitzer design was in 1947 with the Model 1100, nicknamed the "Bullet" or "Bomber Nose," referring to the shape of the window covering the record-changing mechanism.

In addition to the color and glitz of Wurlitzer's jukeboxes, their designs included the visual entertainment of a revealed record-changing mechanism. Other manufacturers did not yet see this as a necessary design element.

Up to now, Wurlitzer's jukebox advertising campaign had focused on the owners/operators of the jukeboxes. In the 1940s, at Fuller's and Capehart's urging, Wurlitzer advertised jukeboxes to the public for the first time, introducing the new "Johnny One Note" logo, officially known as the Sign of the Musical Note. It featured a trumpet-playing musical note with a top hat in front of a spinning record. It appeared on billboards, magazine ads and a wide array of promotional materials given away by Wurlitzer to operators and customers. The logo was so widely publicized that nearly everyone instantly recognized it. With the introduction of stereo, the logo was later modified to include a second "Johnny" as a mirror image. The logo, coupled with the appealing advertising images created by Albert Dorne (1904–1965), served to promote the Model 1015 jukebox to success.

There is evidence to suggest that Wurlitzer jukeboxes had ties to the mafia, much like Wurlitzer faced with its automatic musical instruments of

In 1995, the United States Postal Service issued a first-class stamp to commemorate the fiftieth anniversary of the most popular jukebox in history, the Wurlitzer Model 1015. Although the stamp showed no denomination, it had a twenty-five-cent value. *Courtesy of Greg Dumais.*

the previous era. A cash-based business is an easy place to "skim off" profits before taxes are paid and is the perfect place to launder money. In general, the jukebox manufacturers, including Wurlitzer, did not sell jukeboxes directly to the owners of the bars and restaurants in which they were placed. Instead, they were sold to operators, or middlemen, who would place the boxes, service them and split the take with the owners. In general, the mob was involved directly as operators or through control of some sort of operator association. Through intimidation, sabotage or labor trouble, they acquired a complete monopoly. These same techniques were used for slot, pinball and cigarette vending machines.

Since New York was both the U.S. population center and the center of the entertainment industry in the 1930s, it made sense that the jukebox industry there was a prime target of organized crime. *Billboard* is a trade journal for the entertainment industry that focuses on the rather boring details of finance and technology. Therefore, it is remarkable that an article appeared in the March 13, 1943 issue announcing a new partnership between Wurlitzer and notorious mobster Meyer Lansky:

> *At a trade gathering, several Wurlitzer Company executives presented Meyer Lansky and his associate Ed Smith to the Eastern box operators. Said*

*Wurlitzer official Mike Hammergren: "We know that in Meyer Lansky we have a man who is liked and respected by everyone. We are confident that Wurlitzer's new distributor in New York, New Jersey and Connecticut will make many new friends. Never has Wurlitzer appointed distributors in whom we have more confidence than we have in Meyer Lansky and Eddie Smith."*

A photo appeared in *Billboard* the next month with the caption:

*New distributors celebrate. Appointment of the Manhattan-Simplex Distributing Company, Inc. as Wurlitzer distributor for the Metropolitan New York area was celebrated at a formal opening held recently and attended by about 500 music operators. Pictured above, Wurlitzer General Sales Manager Mike Hammergren congratulates Meyer Lansky, president of the distributing company, as (left to right) Spence Reese, assistant sales manager; Sam Goldberg; Eddie Smith, manager of Manhattan-Simplex, and Carl Johnson, Wurlitzer vice president, look on.*

An article appearing in *Billboard* in 1959 reported that Milton "Mike" G. Hammergren was a former vice-president of Wurlitzer who took over as sales manager in 1949 shortly after Homer Capehart left the company in 1944 to run for successful election as a Republican U.S. senator from Indiana. A formal hearing was held before the Senate Select Committee on Improper Activities in the Labor or Management Field chaired by John McClellan (a Democrat from Arkansas). At the hearing, *Billboard* reported, Hammergren admitted calling on the help of a "friend," Al Goldberg, who had underworld connections. Goldberg arranged for the sale of 550 jukeboxes in Chicago with no money down and no payments for six months. A later arrangement with Meyer Lansky allowed the company to "break through" in the East Coast and set up a new distribution firm there. Goldberg also arranged with Hammergren to enter the St. Louis market. Hammergren said that the Wurlitzer distributor there had been pushed around to the point where he was afraid to leave his hotel room because he "didn't want to be killed." Hammergren testified to similar scenarios in Minneapolis, San Francisco and Detroit. Cleveland proved to be more difficult for the mafia to control, as there was already a strong distributor association run there by William Presser of the Ohio Teamsters Union. When Goldberg tried to do business there, windows were blown out of the store he had rented. Hammergren said violence in the jukebox industry seemed necessary as a matter of survival. "We didn't like force," he said, "but we had to sell jukeboxes."

Meyer Lansky (1902–1983) was a major organized crime figure, known as the "Mob's Accountant." Lansky's business partner was Vincent "Jimmy Blue Eyes" Alo (1904–2001), who was also a notorious mob figure known as "Ed Smith." Both were associated with Charles "Lucky" Luciano (1897–1962), who is regarded as the father of organized crime and considered by many to be the most powerful American mafia boss of all time. In 1947, Lansky sold Simplex Distribution to a group of supposedly non-mob investors and moved his attention to Las Vegas and Cuba. Wurlitzer officially stated that it knew nothing of Lansky's activities until 1947 and that Lansky gave up the franchise as soon as Wurlitzer requested it from him. However, the real reason was that Luciano had just been paroled from prison on the condition that he leave the United States permanently. Instead of returning to his native Sicily as promised, Luciano moved to Cuba to control the casinos and racetracks there and invited Lansky to join him in his new ventures.

Throughout the next few decades following the jukebox's golden years, Wurlitzer steadily released innovative designs. The record selection capacity increased. The audio quality of the jukeboxes became more powerful, and stereo sound replaced mono. The popularity of jukeboxes, however, began to wane somewhat in these years as television took over as the dominant form of entertainment.

Up to 1950, jukeboxes played only 78-rpm records. The playing field changed with the introduction in 1949 of the seven-inch 45-rpm disc; virtually overnight the 78-rpm record was declared obsolete. Seeburg was the first to commit to jukeboxes playing 45s with its M100B model in 1950. Wurlitzer countered with Model 1250, which also incorporated a second tone arm that allowed the playing of "B" sides of records, doubling the selections to 48. In 1952, Wurlitzer produced Model 1500, offering 104 selections. This was achieved by essentially doubling the old Simplex mechanism, creating a "double jukebox," a mechanical nightmare that was compounded by the fact that the machine could mix record speeds: either a 78-rpm or 45-rpm record could be played. The machine adjusted to the correct speed by means of a much-hyped "Wurlimagic Brain." Alternatively, the Model 1500 could be converted to play 33⅓-rpm records.

Wurlitzer's Model 1700 was introduced in 1954, incorporating a completely new record-changing mechanism that accommodated 45-rpm records with 104 selections. From here on, Wurlitzer was once again in the forefront of jukebox design. The advertising slogan used to launch this new model was "Gee, Dad, it's a Wurlitzer!"

This advertisement for Wurlitzer's Model 2910 jukebox remote unit in 1965 was aimed at white audiences; a similar advertisement issued the same year featured African Americans. *Courtesy of North Tonawanda History Museum.*

Wurlitzer observed its centennial in 1956, so to celebrate, the company brought out two new models named "Centennial." Following the styling of automobiles of the era, Wurlitzer advertised the boxes as "a luxurious combination of American hardwoods and embossed metalized Du Pont Mylar. Highly favored today by automobile stylists for interior car trim,

Deutsche Wurlitzer entered the vending machine market in 1963. Their current model W1000 vending machine can be used indoors or outdoors and offers up to sixty selections with optional refrigeration. Another model, the Wurlitzer Deli, features a deep-freeze unit; others dispense hot or cold drinks. *Courtesy of Deutsche Wurlitzer.*

Mylar combines brilliant beauty with amazing wear." The basic Centennial model, Model 1900, had the standard 104 selections; Model 2000 was its first 200-selection machine. With the introduction of Model 2300 in 1959, Wurlitzer decided that revealing the record-changing mechanism was not as important as it had been. Only the top section of the changer, the record in play and the tone arm could now be seen. By 1967, the Americana series completely hid the record-changing mechanism.

Some Wurlitzer jukebox designs of the 1970s sought to imitate home stereo systems using low wooden cabinets with lids that opened to reveal the selection panel. One such model was 1972's Cabaret. Wurlitzer's final American-made jukebox was the Model 3800 of 1974, the last to be made at the North Tonawanda plant. However, the Deutsche Wurlitzer division continued to produce new models, such as the Atlanta, Baltic, Lyric, Tarock, Niagara, X2, Silhouette and Caravelle, among many others. In the 1970s, Deutsche Wurlitzer also produced Carousel models for the American market that played cassette tapes. By the mid-1980s, the nostalgic look of the Wurlitzer jukebox became a symbol of the "good old days," and today, vintage Wurlitzer jukeboxes have become sought-after collector's items. Deutsche Wurlitzer introduced new jukeboxes beginning in 1985 that utilized the latest available technologies. The first compact disc jukebox from Wurlitzer was produced in 1989.

In 1986, Deutsche Wurlitzer introduced the OMT (One More Time) jukebox, an updated version of the iconic Model 1015. In 1989, the OMT jukebox was updated to play either 50 or 100 compact discs. Other designs offered by Deutsche Wurlitzer were the Princess CD jukebox, the Elvis Presley Limited Edition CD jukebox, the Johnny One Note CD jukebox and the Wurlitzer Rainbow, featuring a 120–compact disc mechanism. The final curtain was closed on Wurlitzer jukebox manufacturing on September 5, 2013, with the production of the last Wurlitzer OMT jukebox at the Deutsche Wurlitzer factory. A completely independent company as of January 2013, Deutsche Wurlitzer now focuses exclusively on its other product line: innovative vending machines for the European market.

# 15
# OTHER WURLITZER PRODUCTS

The Rudolph Wurlitzer Company began in 1856 as a musical instrument reseller, and this it continued to do over the years, often rebranding the merchandise since the products were not necessarily manufactured by Wurlitzer. As has been noted in the previous chapters, Wurlitzer was also very much in the forefront of innovation with the research and development of the products they manufactured and sold directly.

Among the many other items sold by Wurlitzer were harmonicas, toys, Victrolas, accordions, furniture, radios, refrigerators, Skee-Ball games and washing machines. These items were met with more or less success, but many were discontinued shortly after their introduction. Overall, Wurlitzer found this diversification to be rather unsuccessful, especially with products that had nothing to do with musical instruments.

The furniture line was discontinued in 1938, but in later years, Wurlitzer entered into contracts with other companies to produce wooden cabinetry for radios and televisions, billiard tables and other items, particularly those made of wood. For a time, accordions were manufactured at the DeKalb plant; beginning in 1968, the DeKalb facility also built home stereo radio phonographs.

## *Refrigerators*

With the decline of sales in the 1920s and 1930s, production of automatic musical instruments ceased until the manufacture of the first Wurlitzer jukebox in 1934. For a brief time, five different models of refrigerators were made by the Wurlitzer-controlled All-American Mohawk Corporation in Chicago beginning about 1929. In 1930, refrigerator manufacturing was transferred to Wurlitzer's North Tonawanda plant. A 1933 advertisement for the Wurlitzer Mohawk "Duo Zone" refrigerator described the feature of the two zones, "one for freezing, one for cooling," and it could freeze ice cubes in less than one hour. And the new refrigerator was affordable: "$9.50 down. You pay us your monthly ice bill of $3.87 for two years and we install it in your home immediately." Wurlitzer discontinued the production of refrigerators in 1937.

MODEL 10

The Wurlitzer Duo Zone refrigerator. *Wurlitzer Company Records, Archives Center, National Museum of American History, Smithsonian Institution.*

## *Radios*

In early 1929, Wurlitzer took over the manufacture of radios with its controlling interest in the All-American Mohawk Corporation. The North Tonawanda factory manufactured tabletop and floor model radios under the Lyric brand beginning about 1930. Lyric radios were considered very high end and retailed in 1929 for $149 for a radio without tubes (to be supplied later by the end retailer) to as much as $425 (about $5,800 in 2014 dollars). Wurlitzer's production of Lyric radios ended in 1938.

For most of the 1930s, Wurlitzer produced several models of Lyric brand radios.
*Courtesy of North Tonawanda History Museum.*

## Skee-Ball

In 1935, Wurlitzer bought the rights to the popular arcade game Skee-Ball. Wurlitzer's version of the cabinet had an Art Deco look and was designed by jukebox artist Paul Fuller. Up to this time, Skee-Ball alleys were operated by an attendant; Wurlitzer's innovation was the addition of a coin slot attachment, eliminating the need for an arcade operator to be present. In 1945, Wurlitzer sold the copyright, patents and exclusive manufacturing rights of Skee-Ball alleys to the Philadelphia Toboggan Company. Retaining its coin slot attachment, Skee-Ball remains a popular amusement park feature today.

## Guitars

In 1966, music store owner Howard Holman used his contacts at the Martin Band Instrument Company, owned by Wurlitzer at that time, to convince Wurlitzer to distribute a line of electric guitars manufactured by Holman's start-up company in Kansas. Wurlitzer thus became the sole distributor of guitars made by the Holman-Woodell Company of Neodesha, Kansas. Part of the agreement was that the guitars would bear the Wurlitzer trademark. The guitar labels listed only Wurlitzer's Elkhart, Indiana location, but the guitars were made in Holman's small factory in Kansas. Three models were made: the Cougar, Wildcat and Gemini, all of which were functionally similar but featured different body shapes. Wurlitzer electric guitars had several innovative features, including true stereo, a pickup blender and a Wurlitzer-designed vibrato tailpiece with its trademark "W" cutout logo. The majority were six-string guitars; only a handful of bass guitars were made. Although the guitars were, and still are, highly regarded by musicians, Wurlitzer ended its association with Holman in 1967, most likely due to problems with the finish on the guitars peeling off. That same year, Wurlitzer then entered into an agreement with Welson Music Industries to produce Wurlitzer guitars at Welson's subsidiary in Italy. The Wurlitzer line was expanded to include semi-hollow body electric guitars, as well as acoustic guitars. In 1969, Wurlitzer stopped selling guitars under its own brand name.

# Wild Ones from Wurlitzer!

*They're here. The first of a broad new line of Wurlitzer Wild Ones –
a new breed of stereo electric guitars bearing the mighty Wurlitzer name!
The Wild Ones are solid. Responsive. Beautiful. More versatile
than anything in their price range has a right to be!*

The Wild Ones are headed for certain success. Each of these American made beauties is backed by Wurlitzer with 109 years of musical instrument experience.

Famous Wurlitzer dealer promotional assistance will help you sell The Wild Ones — and help them become wildly profitable for you!

**Check These Exciting Features:**

STEREO SENSI-TONE PICKUPS ● TUNEMASTER BRIDGE ● VIBRATRON TAIL PIECE ● SLENDER, HARD MAPLE NECK ● ADJUSTABLE TRUSS ROD ● SMARTLY STYLED FINGERBOARD WITH INLAID PEARL POSITION MARKERS AND BOUND EDGES ● NICKEL SILVER FRETS ● EXCLUSIVE WURLITZER AGRAFFE ● CHOICE OF THREE POPULAR COLORS IN EACH MODEL ● SMARTLY STYLED, COLORFULLY PLUSH-LINED ROYALITE CASES.

*COUGAR    GEMINI    WILDCAT*

## WURLITZER
DEPT. NO. 9610
ELKHART, INDIANA 46515

Wurlitzer introduced a line of electric guitars in 1966 named Cougar, Wildcat and Gemini. This advertisement from *Music Trades* shows the three models, each featuring a vibrato tailpiece with the trademark "W" cutout logo. *From the collection of the Public Library of Cincinnati and Hamilton County.*

# *The Orgatron*

The Orgatron electrostatic reed organ was first produced in 1934 by Frederick Albert Hoschke. This instrument was an electronic organ that produced pitches by means of a fan blowing air over a set of free reeds; the pitches were then captured electronically to produce musical tones. The Orgatron was manufactured by the Everett Piano Company from 1935 to 1941. After World War II, Everett was acquired by Wurlitzer, which resumed production in 1945, discontinuing the instrument in the mid-1960s.

## *The Side Man*

Although the first drum machine available for sale was the Chamberlin Rhythmate in 1949, very few were ever built. Ten years later, Wurlitzer released its own electro-mechanical drum machine called the Side Man, the first widely available, commercially produced drum machine. The Side Man

The cover of the June 1960 issue of *Music Trades* featured Wurlitzer's innovative Side Man drum machine. *From the collection of the Public Library of Cincinnati and Hamilton County.*

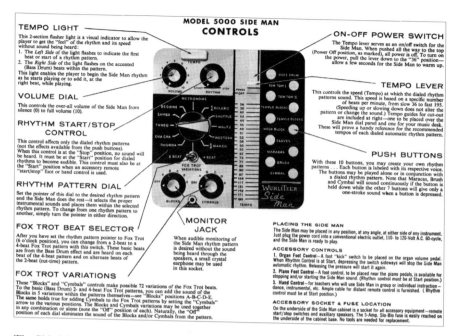

The Side Man produced percussion effects by means of vacuum tube oscillators controlled by a mechanical commutator that determined the rhythm patterns. *Courtesy of Jeff Weiler.*

was a success for Wurlitzer and was produced in several models between 1959 and 1965 that sold for about $400 in a cabinet with a choice of walnut, cherry or mahogany. An innovative product, the Side Man used a disc with electrical contacts spaced to create various rhythmic patterns (tango, rhumba, waltz, fox trot and so forth). An arm positioned above the rotating disc converted the patterns to electrical signals that were then fed to circuitry containing vacuum tubes to create ten preset drum sounds. Although the disc rotated at a constant speed, the pickup arm could be moved away from or closer to the center of the disc to vary the tempo. It was possible to manually trigger ten additional sounds, including bass drum, maracas and so forth, by pressing buttons. The Side Man enjoyed some success among home organists and performers, who used them to accompany their onstage performances.

# *The Orbit III Synthesizer*

In 1971, Wurlitzer introduced the Orbit III, a basic monophonic synthesizer, included as the third manual on several different Wurlitzer home organ models beginning with Model 4037 and others in the years following (Models 4373, 4573, 555 and others). It had a basic envelope that included attack and sustain, a filter of sorts (called "wah-wah"), and a "modulator" with settings for rate and "deviation" (depth). The Orbit III had ten presets (Reed, Brass, String, Banjo, Harpsichord, Electro Piano, Vibes, Xylophone and Piano). Each synthesis function could be completely toggled on and off via push button, and the sound of the synthesizer was modified by a row of organ-style buttons affecting the timbre and the range. The organs typically also included drumbeats and a cassette player/recorder.

# AFTERWORD

Wurlitzer President R.C. Rolfing, writing in the introduction to the company's centennial booklet, *Wurlitzer World of Music: 100 Years of Musical Achievement*, provided this summation of the Wurlitzer Company's philosophy:

> *Wurlitzer is the name that means music to millions all over the world just as the name Ford means automobile, Bell means telephone and Singer means sewing machine. And for much the same sound reason. Each of these men, in his turn, recognized vast, potential markets for basic products of superior quality. And while Rudolph Wurlitzer did not invent musical instruments any more than Henry Ford invented automobiles, both had the vision to supply the need with popularly-priced products theretofore restricted to a privileged few.*

It is interesting to imagine how Rudolph Wurlitzer would have viewed the way his company developed over the years following his death. No doubt he would have been very proud of the success of the various automatic instruments the company both sold and created. The Mighty Wurlitzer theater organ helped further propel the family name to worldwide renown. Even today, most harpists know of the wonderful sound and durability of Wurlitzer harps even if they've never had the opportunity to play one. Others fondly recall playing or listening to a home, church or school Wurlitzer piano, a reliable and serviceable instrument. And many people the world over associate the name Wurlitzer with jukeboxes and good times.

# Afterword

The company's embracing of the electronic age would likely have mystified Rudolph, and he would have been surprised at the market takeover of both acoustic and electronic instruments by Asian manufacturers in recent years. He would likely have been proud of the fact that the company was led by only two generations of Wurlitzers for a remarkable 116 years. It is interesting to contemplate what he would have thought of his company being bought 150 years after its founding by a prominent guitar manufacturer in Nashville. And he likely would have marveled at the vending machines currently being made by Deutsche Wurlitzer in his homeland, in an area not far from where he acquired his first musical instruments for resale. It can be said that, with its "return" to Germany in the form of Deutsche Wurlitzer, the Rudolph Wurlitzer Company has come full circle.

# Bibliography

Almind, Gert. "Wurlitzer Jukeboxes." Unpublished manuscript, October 2013.

Asbury, Herbert. *The Barbary Coast: An Informal History of the San Francisco Underworld.* Garden City, NY: Garden City Publishing Co., 1933.

Bopp, Ron. *The American Carousel Organ: An Illustrated Encyclopedia.* St. Cloud, MN: R. Bopp, 1998.

Botts, Rick. *A Complete Identification Guide to the Wurlitzer Jukebox.* Des Moines, IA: Jukebox Collector Newsletter, 1990.

Bowers, Q. David. *Encyclopedia of Automatic Musical Instruments.* Vestal, NY: Vestal Press, 1972.

———. *Put Another Nickel In: A History of Coin-operated Pianos and Orchestrions.* New York: Bonanza Books, 1966.

Carson, Berry. "Electric Pianos." *Keyboard* 19 (December 1993): 154–56.

Carter, Denny. *Henry Farny.* New York: Watson-Guptill, 1978.

*Cincinnati City Guide and Business Directory, For the Year 1870: Containing a Classified List of All Trades, Professions, And Pursuits In the City of Cincinnati, Alphabetically Arranged.* Cincinnati, OH: Chas. F. Wilstach & Co., 1870.

# Bibliography

Cincinnati Federal Writers' Project. *They Built A City: 150 Years of Industrial Cincinnati*. Cincinnati, OH: Cincinnati Post, 1938.

Cist, Charles. *Sketches and Statistics of Cincinnati in 1851*. Cincinnati, OH: Wm. H. Moore & Co., 1851.

Crandall, Rick. "J.W. Whitlock and His Automatic Harp." *Musical Box Society International Technical Bulletin* (Spring/Summer 1985): 21–61.

Detroy, Michael A. "Cincinnati's Albee-Emery Wurlitzer." *Theatre Organ: Journal of the American Theatre Organ Society* 18, no. 3 (June–July 1976): 17–19.

Deutsche Wurlitzer GmbH. "Wurlitzer." http://www.wurlitzer.de.

Ederveen, Regina. "A Century of Wurlitzer Harps: 1909–2009." *American Harp Journal* 22, no. 1 (Summer 2009): 56–61.

Fairfield, John H. *Known Violin Makers*. Cape Coral, FL: Virtuoso, 1983.

Fucini, Joseph J., and Suzy Fucini. "Rudolph Wurlitzer, 1831–1914: Wurlitzer Instruments." In *Entrepreneurs: The Men and Women Behind Famous Brand Names and How They Made It*. Boston: G.K. Hall & Co., 1985.

Gelfand, Janelle. "Mighty Wurlitzer Has a New Home." http://www.cincinnati.com.

Graham, Lloyd. "The Story of the Rudolph Wurlitzer Family and Business." Unpublished manuscript, May 25, 1955.

Greve, Charles Theodore. *Centennial History of Cincinnati and Representative Citizens*. Chicago: Biographical Pub. Co., 1904.

Hair, James T. *J.C.W. Bailey & Co.'s Chicago City Directory for the Year 1865–6*. Chicago: John C.W. Bailey, 1865.

Haller, Charles R. "Wurlitzer." In *German-American Business Biographies: High Finance and Big Business*. Asheville, NC: Money Tree Imprints, 2001.

Hathaway, Terry. "The Wurlitzer Family Grave Sites in Spring Grov Cemetery, Cincinnati, Ohio." http://www.mechanicalmusicpress.com.

Haynes, Danielle. "Wurlitzer: A Symbol of Industry." *Tonawanda News,* February 6, 2012.

Hearn, Lafcadio. *Ye Giglampz.* Cincinnati, OH: Giglampz Pub. Co., 1874.

Historical Society of the Tonawandas. *Tonawanda and North Tonawanda.* Charleston, SC: Arcadia Publishing, 2011.

Hope-Jones, Robert. *Recent Developments of Organ Building: Being a Lecture Delivered before the National Association of Organists at the Auditorium, Ocean Grove, N.J., U.S.A. August 6ᵗʰ, 1910 (abbreviated).* North Tonawanda, NY: Rudolph Wurlitzer Co., 1910.

"The House of Wurlitzer, 1856–1906." *Music Trades* (December 1906): 61–68.

John C.W. Bailey & Co. *John C.W. Bailey's Chicago City Directory, For the Year 1866–7.* Chicago: John C.W. Bailey, 1866.

———. *John C.W. Bailey's Chicago City Directory, For the Year 1867–8.* Chicago: John C.W. Bailey, 1867.

Junchen, David L. *The Wurlitzer Pipe Organ: An Illustrated History.* [Indianapolis, IN?]: American Theatre Organ Society, 2005.

Kaufmann, Preston J. *Encyclopedia of the American Theatre Organ.* Vol. 3. Pasadena, CA: Showcase Publications, 1995.

Kenny, Daniel J. *Illustrated Cincinnati: A Pictorial Hand-book of the Queen City, Comprising Its Architecture, Manufacture, Trade; Its Social, Literary, Scientific, and Charitable Institutions; Its Churches, Schools and Colleges; and All Other Principal Points of Interest to the Visitor and Resident, Together with an Account of the Most Attractive Suburbs, by D.J. Kenny. Illustrated with Over Three Hundred and Twenty Engravings and a New and Complete Map.* Cincinnati, OH: R. Clarke, 1875.

Klauprecht, Emil. *German Chronicle in the History of the Ohio Valley and Its Capital City, Cincinnati, in Particular.* Bowie, MD: Heritage Books, 1992. (German language original published 1864.)

Kuettner, Al. "Emery Theatre Organ Dedicated." *Theatre Organ: Journal of the American Theatre Organ Society* 20, no. 1 (January/February 1978): 43–45.

*The Lakeside Annual Directory of the City of Chicago, 1901.* Chicago: Chicago Directory Co., 1901.

Landon, John W. *Behold the Mighty Wurlitzer: The History of the Theatre Pipe Organ.* Westport, CT: Greenwood Press, 1983.

———. "Part III Musical Instruments: 10. Keyboard Instruments: Wurlitzer Organ." In *Continuum Encyclopedia of Popular Music of the World* 2 (July 2003): 321–22.

"Lansky-Smith New Wurlitzer N.Y., N.J., Conn. Distribs," *Billboard*, March 13, 1943, 59.

Leonard, Lewis Alexander, ed. "Rudolph H. Wurlitzer." In *Greater Cincinnati and Its People: A History.* Vol. 4. New York: Lewis Historical Pub. Co., 1927.

Letter from Farny Wurlitzer to Art Reblitz, February 26, 1962. http://www.mechanicalmusicpress.com.

Ludwig, Corinna. "Rudolph Wurlitzer, 1831–1914." In *Immigrant Entrepreneurship: German-American Business Biographies 1720 to the Present,* edited by Giles R. Hoyt. German Historical Institute. Last modified June 26, 2013. http:// www.immigrantentrepreneurship.org/entry.php?rec=45.

Lynch, Vincent. *Jukebox: The Golden Age.* Berkeley, CA: Lancaster-Miller, 1981.

McCracken, Harold. *Portrait of the Old West: With a Biographical Check List of Western Artists.* New York: McGraw-Hill, 1952.

"Meeting Farny Reginald Wurlitzer." http://www.mechanicalmusicpress.com.

Mountain, Ken. *The Birth of a Jukebox.* http://www.nthistorymuseum.org/Collections/wurjuke.html.

*Musical Courier: A Weekly Journal Devoted to Music and the Music Trades.* 1883–1961.

*Music Trades.* (1890–present).

Neal, Donna Zellner, ed. *North Tonawanda: The Lumber City.* Bloomington, IN: Trafford Publishing, 2007.

"New Distributors Celebrate." *Billboard*, April 10, 1943, 87.

Newspaper Cartoonists Association of Cincinnati. *A Gallery of Pen Sketches in Black and White of Cincinnatians As We See 'Em.* Cincinnati, OH: A. McNeill, 1905.

Palkovic, Mark. "The Harps of the Rudolph Wurlitzer Company." *American Harp Journal* 10, no. 3 (Summer 1986): 16–26.

Paul Mensch Directory Co. *Chicago Central Business and Office Building Directory.* Chicago: Paul Mensch Directory Co., 1899.

Pearce, Christopher. *Vintage Jukeboxes.* Edison, NJ: Chartwell Books, 1988.

"The Philipps Pianella a.k.a. the Wurlitzer PianOrchestra." http://www.mechanicalmusicpress.com.

"The Philipps Pianella and the Wurlitzer PianOrchestra." http://www.mechanicalmusicpress.com.

*Pierce Piano Atlas.* 11th ed. Albuquerque, NM: Larry E. Ashley, 2003.

Rasmussen, Gary. "House of Wurlitzer." *AMICA Bulletin* (March/April 2010): 86–99.

Reblitz, Arthur A. *The Golden Age of Automatic Musical Instruments: Remarkable Music Machines and Their Stories.* Woodsville, NH: Mechanical Music Press, 2001.

Rensch, Roslyn. *Harps and Harpists.* Revised ed. Bloomington: Indiana University Press, 2007.

Roell, Craig H. *The Piano in America, 1890–1940.* Chapel Hill: University of North Carolina Press, 1989.

*Rookwood VIII & Keramics 1998: Featuring Important Consignments From the Family of Carl Schmidt, An Important Midwestern Collector, The Family of Mary Nourse And Other Important Collections.* Cincinnati, OH: Cincinnati Art Galleries, 1998. Auction catalogue.

Rudolph Wurlitzer & Bro. *Band, Reed and String Instruments: Catalogue and Descriptive Price-List,* 17th ed. Cincinnati, OH: Rudolph Wurlitzer & Bro., [1880?].

———. *Musical Merchandise and Strings: Catalogue and Descriptive Price List,* 19th ed. Cincinnati, OH: Rudolph Wurlitzer & Bro., [1880?].

Rudolph Wurlitzer Co. *Band Instruments, Drums, Fifes, Clarionets, Flutes, Piccolos and Trimmings: Illustrated Catalogue and Price List,* 30th ed. Cincinnati, OH: Rudolph Wurlitzer Co., [1890?].

———. *A Book of Recipes Covering Three Generations of the Farny and Wurlitzer Family and the Wives of Present Business Associates.* North Tonawanda, NY: Rudolph Wurlitzer Co., 1956.

———. *Masterpieces of the Great Violin Makers,* 2nd ed. New York: Rudolph Wurlitzer Co., 1918.

———. *Musical Instruments, Wurlitzer Catalog no. 47.* Cincinnati: Rudolph Wurlitzer Co., 1901.

———. *Presenting the Wurlitzer Reproducing Residence Organ.* Goodwood, Australia: W.A. Crowle Ltd., 1975 reprint.

———. *A Visit to Wurlitzer* (videorecording). 39 min. Buffalo, NY: McLarty Films, ca. 1950.

———. *Wurlitzer Automatic Musical Instruments Manufactured by the Rudolph Wurlitzer Co.,* [1906?].

———. *Wurlitzer Automatic Musical Instruments Manufactured by the Rudolph Wurlitzer Co.,* [1909?].

———. *The Wurlitzer Harp: The Costliest Harp in the World*. Cincinnati, OH: The Rudolph Wurlitzer Co., [1916?].

———. *The Wurlitzer Harp: The World's Best Harp*. New York: The Rudolph Wurlitzer Co., 1924.

———. *Wurlitzer Musical Instruments and Supplies*, [catalogue no. 110], Cincinnati, OH: Rudolph Wurlitzer Co., 1918.

———. *Wurlitzer Musical Merchandise Catalogue for Dealers, Number 97*. Cincinnati, OH: Rudolph Wurlitzer Co., 1910.

———. *Wurlitzer World of Music, 1856–1956: 100 Years of Musical Achievement*. Chicago: Rudolph Wurlitzer Co., 1956.

"The Rudolph Wurlitzer Co." In *Cincinnati: The Queen City Newspaper Reference Book*. Cincinnati, OH: Cuvier Press Club, 1914.

Segrave, Kerry. *Jukeboxes: An American Social History*. Jefferson, NC: McFarland & Co., 2002.

"Senate Racket Hearing Open As Headlines Lash Industry." *Billboard*, February 16, 1959, 80, 82.

Skolle, John. *The Lady of the Casa: The Biography of Helene V.B. Wurlitzer*. Santa Fe, NM: Rydal Press, 1959.

Thiele, John. *When the Mighty Wurlitzer Reigned in the Regent*. Campbelltown, South Australia: Hyde Park Press, 2011.

Vitz, Robert C. *The Queen and the Arts: Cultural Life in Nineteenth-Century Cincinnati*. Kent, OH: Kent State University Press, 1989.

Wehmeier, Ron. "Not Just Another Wurlitzer Update." *Theatre Organ: Journal of the American Theatre Organ Society* 35, no. 5 (September/October 1993): 8–11.

———. "Rebirth in Cincinnati: From the Albee to the Music Hall." *Theatre Organ: Journal of the American Theatre Organ Society* 52, no. 4 (July/August 2010): 30–37.

*Williams' Cincinnati Directory: Embracing a Full Alphabetical Record of the Names of the Inhabitants of Cincinnati, a Business Directory, Municipal Record, And a Map of Cincinnati: Also, Directories of Covington and Newport, etc.: June, 1872.* Cincinnati, OH: Williams & Co., 1872.

Wurlitzer Co. *Supplementary Catalog, Wurlitzer Music for Theatres.* North Tonawanda, NY: Wurlitzer Co., 1963 reprint.

Wurlitzer, Farny Reginald. Letter to William Griess Jr. December 11, 1951. Private collection.

"Wurlitzer Jukebox 1015." In *Icons of Design: The 20th Century.* New York: Prestel, 2000.

"Wurlitzer Juke Box: A Victim of Changing Times." *North Tonawanda News,* April 6, 1974.

Wurlitzer, Leonie, and Marguerite Strobel. *A Book of Recipes Covering Three Generations of the Farny and Wurlitzer Family.* Privately printed, 1925.

Yelton, Geary. "Dawn of the Drum Machine." *Electronic Musician* 26, no. 12 (December 2010): 16.

# INDEX

# About the Author

Mark Palkovic has held the position of librarian at the College-Conservatory of Music Library at the University of Cincinnati since 1981. A graduate of Ohio University majoring in music history, Palkovic has also served as associate editor of the *American Harp Journal*. He is a longtime member of the Cincinnati Men's Chorus and has performed with a wide variety of local and regional musical organizations.

*Visit us at*
www.historypress.net

*This title is also available as an e-book*